CW01625389

An eBay™ Life for Me

Tips and Advice on How to Sell Online Successfully

Dawn Wilkinson

Paperback Edition First Published in Great Britain in 2021 by Dawn Wilkinson

eBook Edition First Published in Great Britain in 2021 by Dawn Wilkinson

ISBN: 978-1-913438-54-8

aSys Publishing

Flutterbuys123

Always Bargains There Will Be!

A Collection of Tips and Advice from a Top-Rated eBay Seller

Dawn Wilkinson

Flutterbuys123

Feedback score over 91,000
Positive Feedback (last 12 months): 100%

Registered as a business seller

eBay Top-rated seller:

One of eBay's most reputable sellers.

Consistently delivers outstanding customer service

www.ebay.co.uk/usr/flutterbuys123

www.ebaystores.co.uk/flutterbuys123

Examples of recent feedback received

Thank you for selling on eBay market place, trusted seller 100%positive feedback

Excellent seller quick delivery will buy again thanks

Excellent and reliable. the item was well packaged and it was delivered very quick. I would highly recommend them.

Very happy customer, seller highly recommended, very accurate and honest seller.

Very quick delivery good quality would definitely buy from you again.

WOW!! ⚡Lightning delivery & Fab item. 5☆☆☆☆☆. Seller highly recommended. Thank you

A1 Ebayer as described

This item confirms what I had already heard - this eBay seller is superb!

Fast delivery, item as described excellent service.

Acknowledgements

Firstly, I should like to thank all my wonderful family and friends who have supported me over the years. Special thanks go to:

My partner, Gary, who regularly scours the internet helping to look for stock for me, then collecting it! He is so understanding too when I have boxes stacked high! I often hear him say "I hope you know what you're doing?!" I have also caused Gary much stress while writing and re-writing this book. I would print my pages off with every re-write causing him to ask "How much b****y ink are you going through?! This book is going to end up costing us a fortune!"

My mam, Maureen, who has always supported me whatever I do. I've lost count how many times she has helped me source stock. We have met some strange and wonderful people while collecting it! And a big thank you to her too for also offering me much needed storage space over the years!

My sister, Katie, who is now an eBay™ seller too! Katie has also offered storage space and helped me collect stock over the years. We have had many trips together to the local cash and carry stores.

My nephew Ethan, and nieces Evie, Daisy, and Thea. They have all, at some time, helped sort stock out with me. I have to say they have all been a great help at times!

To all my wonderful suppliers, many of whom have become good friends, with special thanks to Michael and Sue. In the early days of selling, the stock I bought from them really helped boost my sales and build my business. Brian, from Tynemouth Station has also been a regular supplier – for which I am really thankful. I also need to mention Selwin who has also been a regular supplier of stock over the last few years.

All of my customers who have continued to support me by buying from my eBay shop. There are so many reputable Top-Rated Sellers on eBay and I know I have many returning customers, which I really appreciate.

A huge thanks to all the Royal Mail staff with a special acknowledgement to Nick (my regular postman) who collected my parcels from me daily, for numerous years.

Special thanks also to my friends Karen, Adrienne, Sue, and Wynne who read my first draft of this book and gave useful feedback to help improve the content.

Also, a massive 'thank you' to John Hamer for his help. I have had the idea of writing this book for a number of years, however, meeting John spurred me on to finally manifest this book. I am very grateful for the knowledge he has shared with me, as an already established author, in order to help me complete this book.

Foreword

Dawn has always been a big inspiration to me, mainly because she is my big sister and my only sibling. I have followed in her online selling footsteps, which is something I never had thought I would have attempted. However, due to my busy life of running a home and child caring, it has been the perfect means of making a good income. The beauty of which is I can list items in times that suit me, when children are at school or in bed. My eBay™ shop is called Krafty_Keepsakes and although not in the same vein as Dawn's eBay™ shop (Flutterbuys123), her advice was invaluable towards enabling me to navigate this new successful adventure. She's taught me how to source stock and gave advice on how to deal with customers queries. As I said, my products are totally different to Dawn's, I enjoy selling creative items such as wedding favours, novelty gifts and personalised items. Dawn's extensive knowledge of eBay™ is useful no matter what products someone chooses to sell. Dawn and I frequently visited 'cash and carrys' together and we have shared many interesting and funny stories relating to our eBay™ experiences.

Dawn has always put 100% commitment into anything she does, I can fully recommend her book as the tips and advice are what has helped me to have the confidence of selling online. Being an online seller gives you the freedom to work the hours you want and best of all you are your own boss, which I find extremely appealing.

Katie Stark

Contents

"Dream big. Start small. But most of all, start."

Simon Sinek, motivational speaker

1
Introduction

The purpose of this book is to provide tips on how to buy and sell online successfully. Whether you want to make some extra cash from decluttering or simply to go 'full steam ahead' and start your own business online, I will help you gain knowledge from my own extensive experience, to help you make money.

In this book I will share my experiences of selling online, including some amusing stories, tips, and advice on how to make money in your spare time or turn it into a full-time job. I also encourage you to search for videos on *www.youtube.com* at the end of each chapter and search for related content. I will explain on a very basic level, however, sometimes learning using a visual tool for yourself can help simplify things. I am also happy to email you an up-to-date list of recommended videos to watch upon request.

You will learn how to list an item and use keywords in order to reach more potential customers. I will also include advice on how to source stock and other useful tips to help build your online sales. This book aims to help the beginner and help you begin your own successful online business. I will focus on the basics of what you need to know and how to develop your own business to suit your needs as you go along.

A question I often get asked is… "*How much money do you make in a week?*"

I would never dream of asking people what their salary is but for some reason people seem to think that online sellers would be happy to answer this question. I normally answer *"it varies, depending on how many items I have listed."* This is true. The more items you list the more potential buyers you will attract. The more time you invest in researching stock the more likely you are to stock items which are going to make you a good profit. The more time you are willing to invest, the more money you can potentially make.

I began selling online in 2004. It began as a way of decluttering the house when we were moving. I made enough money from selling on eBay™ to pay our solicitor's bill. I would then scour car boot sales and charity shops for bargains to sell on at a profit. At this point I was working full time and selling online was just my hobby. Some of the other staff I worked with even began selling their own items online when I told them what I was doing in my spare time. They followed my advice and were soon making money for themselves and would share their success stories with me.

Before long, as my sales were increasing, I was going to the post office every day with a bag full of parcels. I got to know the Post Office Staff very well!

For a while it felt as though I had the best job in the world. It felt just like my second home and honestly did not feel like work at all. However, over time circumstances changed, and I no longer felt this way. I knew in my heart it was time to move on.

At the same time I was feeling unsettled in my job, I received a notification from PayPal™ stating my gross payments were approaching £4500 (which was the limit before declaring as a business). I was advised that if I was to continue receiving money through PayPal™ I may be asked to change my account from personal to a business account. I knew I couldn't have this as a second income as I would pay more tax and wasn't sure it would be worth all the work involved. I also didn't know how much longer I could carry on in my employment. And when I started dreading going back to work on a Monday morning this was a bad sign. I talked it over with my partner (Gary) about leaving my job and becoming an online business seller. Gary is a born worrier, so I wasn't expecting him to tell me to go for it. We had a mortgage to pay, and not having the security of two regular wages I knew would cause him concern. However he said if you think you can do it, just do it!

So, I set myself a target to save my wages over the next few months of employment and have that money in the bank as an emergency fund. During the early days I knew I would need to re-invest most of the money I made, back into the business. I did not tell my boss about my plans but I went to work every day and got on with my job even though I hated it by this time.

As time went by I knew I was growing more miserable in my employment and selling online was a more exciting prospect for me. The 'Del Boy' in me had definitely been unleashed and I loved the idea of being my own boss. I found no excitement in working for a boss anymore.

I made the decision to leave my employment in 2007 and registered as a self-employed sole trader.

I changed my online selling ID to Flutterbuys123 as I liked the sound of it and I also thought of a short and snappy slogan for my business cards...

Flutterbuys123

Always bargains there will be!

It was so exciting knowing that I was my own boss. No more negotiating time off, no more following orders, no more stress!

For the first time in my life I really enjoyed working! Every day offered new opportunities. I enjoyed learning about my new venture. Spending hours learning and researching. I already had knowledge of accountancy and book-keeping so that was a big help!

Getting up every morning with excitement was a fantastic feeling I had never experienced before. I visited stores and Cash and Carry outlets to build up my stock. I met some lovely people at car boot sales and markets. I gradually built up a list of suppliers and spent many hours researching what type of stock to acquire. I was now working 7 days a week but it did not feel like work. I enjoyed every minute of it, I didn't want a day off!

I loved the feeling of securing a successful sale and making a profit! I made mistakes along the way but learnt to not make the same errors again. Calculating postage costs and online selling fees correctly was so important.

Family and friends also helped out by supplying me with used jiffy envelopes and boxes to help keep my packaging costs down. A strict budget was in place to ensure my business grew at a steady and manageable pace.

When I first began self-employment I reinvested all my income into buying more stock and before too long I had 4000 items listed and was making a steady income. Obviously, it does take time to build-up to that level of stock and you need to spend many hours sourcing and listing that stock.

Remember, the saying 'Buy Low, Sell High!' I do think however that an item is only worth what someone is willing to pay for it. Reasonable and competitive pricing will deliver successful sales.

Even after all my years of experience I am still learning. The purpose of this book is to share my experiences and hopefully inspire you to see how simple it is to make some extra money or even change your career. If you want to break free from miserable employment and be your own boss, you can do it! It's not always easy, you will need to put in long hours, especially when you first start. The freedom of eventually becoming your own boss is well worth it in the end though.

When I first registered as a sole trader online I read Alan Sugar's autobiography and also Duncan Bannatyne's book called 'Anyone can do it: My Story.' These two books are very inspiring reads! The quote below from Duncan Bannatyne explains it all…

"Life is too fragile and valuable to be spent doing something you hate."

I also like these inspiring quotes…

"There's no elevator to success. You have to take the stairs."

"If you don't build your dream, someone will hire you to build theirs."

So… let's get cracking and make some money!

“The entrepreneurial instinct is in you. You can’t learn it, you can’t buy it, you can’t put it in a bottle. It’s just there and it comes out.”

Alan Sugar

2

Getting Started

Induction

It is far more productive for you to browse the website you intend to use (I use eBay™) and get used to the layout rather than my going into lots of specific details in this book. The reason for this is that websites regularly update layouts and procedures, so any input from me may be completely out of date by the time you read this book!

I refer to this as your induction period. When you start any new job you normally have an induction day in order to familiarise yourself with the building you are working in and also company processes and policies. It makes complete sense to familiarise yourself with the website you are going to use and maintain an up-to-date knowledge of the sites policies etc.

Buying Basics

I would advise spending a few hours getting to know the website and reading the help pages to really get you 'settled in' before you start selling. I personally find eBay™ is a very user-friendly site. If you have never bought anything from the eBay™ site before, I recommend scrolling down to the bottom of the Home Page where you will find a link 'Buying basics.' Click on this link and read all the information available. I would also advise buying a few items through the website you have chosen, to help you get used to the procedures. You will also need to build-up your feedback score. I will go into the importance of feedback later in this book.

So, to begin, search for items that interest you and click on 'add to my watch list.' This enables you to see how the page is laid out. It will also help you keep an eye on other sellers' items and the final prices they achieved.

Then bid on a few items to see how the auction process works. You will need to build your feedback up as a buyer before you can start selling. Check the 'Help and contact' page to find out your seller limits, as their policies can change.

eBay™ have an excellent support team who are available for online chats. Any problem you come up against refer straight back to the 'Help and Contact' link.

When I began selling on eBay™ I had not read any books on how to sell online. I simply learnt along the way and followed the instructions available. But after selling for a short time I did eventually read a few books about selling online for tips and advice. The books I read went into great detail about the policies relevant at the time on eBay™. However, as I mentioned earlier, the site will often update policies and create new aspects to improve its usability. Therefore, I will not include full details as this information may well change frequently and in addition would be really daunting for a complete beginner. Just as when you learn to drive, your driving instructor would never ask you to drive on a motorway on day one! Selling online is similar to learning to drive. Master the basics first and then progress gradually as you feel comfortable. Once you start selling, I guarantee you will find it extremely easy.

Registration

In order to buy and/or sell online, and haven't already done so, you will need to register on the website you are going to use.

It is really simple to register on most sites. Simply click on the 'create account' link and follow the instructions.

There are numerous online selling websites you can use. I personally use the well-known, most popular online auction site eBay™.

My advice would be to browse all the online selling websites and decide which one best suits your needs. Here are a few websites you might want to investigate . . .

www.etsy.com

www.shpock.com

www.gumtree.com

www.vinted.co.uk

www.ebid.net

www.amazon.co.uk

www.onbuy.com

User ID Name

You will obviously need to choose a user ID name. Think about this carefully, although you can change it if you wish, at a later date. If you are starting a business and opening an online shop, try to pick a name that reflects the type of products you are intending to sell.

For example, if I was to open an online shop selling pet products my shop could be called . . .

Dawn's Pet Supplies

I know that's not very imaginative, but it is just an example!

PayPal™

You may also need a PayPal™ account. PayPal™ is very easy to understand and use. Simply follow the instructions in order to register your bank card details. When you first start selling online, sometimes PayPal™ will set limits on your account which they then increase as time goes by. Browse through your PayPal™ account and get used to the layout. Just to reiterate, it is a very easy site to use.

If you have any problems with registration or verifying your PayPal™ account there are online help options for customer support.

To set up your PayPal™ account you will need:

Email address—this email address needs to be linked to your online seller account so when someone buys an item the money will be directed to your PayPal™ account.

Credit card or debit card (bank account details) to be registered to your PayPal™ account. This is needed because if you buy anything on eBay™ and haven't got sufficient funds in your PayPal™ account, the extra amount needed for payment can be taken directly from the card you have on record.

Telephone number

When you first open a PayPal™ account you will need to select the personal account. If you decide later that you are going to sell as a business you will need to change your account to a business account.

You will need to verify your PayPal™ account and you will receive instructions of how to do this from PayPal™.

PayPal™ is the preferred choice of payment method for most sellers online. In the early days I did have regular customers who preferred to pay by postal order or cheque. However, over the years this has gradually decreased and now I very rarely get payments via these methods.

PayPal™ is a fast payment method. The money is instantly transferred to your account most times. Occasionally you may have a payment pending if someone has paid you via echeque. Do not post your item until the echeque has cleared.

Once you receive money in your PayPal™ account you can transfer any amount over £50 to your bank account with no fees. If you wish to transfer a sum of money to your account under £50 you will be charged a fee by PayPal™. The amount will be shown in your account before you agree to the transfer. You can also send money using the 'family and friends' option and incur no fees.

PayPal™ is constantly improving its website and over the years has added many more features. It has Monthly Sales reports which may be printed or downloaded every month.

PayPal™ Fees

Every payment you receive through PayPal™ will incur a fee. All PayPal™ users are automatically allocated a particular fee scale on their payments. To see the latest charges, you will need to refer to PayPal™.

For many years I was paying the set fee charges and then one day I was reading a book about selling on eBay™ and I discovered the micropayments option on PayPal™. This enables you, when receiving amounts of £9.38 or less (at the time of writing, but please check this limit before proceeding) to pay a smaller fee by signing up for micropayments. This will save you quite a lot of money on your PayPal™ fees, overall.

A standard account (which you will automatically be allocated to) used to charge me 3.4% + 20p per transaction.

However, the micropayments account charged me only 5% +5p per transaction so I immediately contacted PayPal™ and signed up for a micropayments account. After the first month alone, I found I had saved myself £75 on my PayPal™ fees. Over the course of one year that's a £900 saving! That book was the best £7.99 I ever spent!

Please remember though, micropayments will only work out cheaper than the standard PayPal™ fees if you are mainly selling items for under £9.38.

Your PayPal™ fee is immediately deducted from your payment received so you never have a bill to pay for your PayPal™ fees.

Managed Payments

eBay™ has recently started managing payments for sellers. This does actually simplify things as you can choose to have your payments paid directly into your bank account daily or weekly. The advantage of this is that your selling fees have already been deducted so you are paid what you have earned (after fees) straight into your bank account.

The Seller Hub

I would advise navigating the Seller Hub currently used on eBay™. The hub includes all your selling information. There will be some links that you will not need to use when you first begin. However, as your sales grow and you become more familiar with the processes, you will probably use more of the facilities available in the seller hub.

The seller hub is a recent addition to the eBay™ site and is very easy to navigate. It comprises of the following sections:

Overview—Includes a simplified view of your listings, orders, sales graphs, shortcuts, selling tools, promotional offers, feedback and basically everything you need to run your business smoothly. This is a useful way to see all relevant information on one page.

Orders—All completed orders awaiting dispatch are listed in this section. As you complete each order click the 'mark as dispatched' option in the drop down list next to your order.

Listings—Use this section to view your live listings. Your unsold items will also be available in this section if you wish to relist them.

Marketing—Use this section to manage your marketing activity and to start a markdown sale and issue voucher codes for potential customers.

Performance—This section includes sales graphs to help you monitor your sales and to see full details of how your business is performing.

Payments—Includes details of all transactions, payouts and reports. It will also show how much you will be receiving in your bank account daily.

Research—This section includes tools to help with product research. Listing improvements and restocking advice is also available.

Reports—Generate and download up-to-date reports that reflect the state of your orders and listings.

Tips To Remember

Induction Day

> **Browse the site you wish to use, in order to get used to the layout.**
>
> **Take time to read the site's information and policy pages.**

Think of a suitable ID username.

Build your feedback as a buyer before starting to sell.

Set up a PayPal™ account or sign up for Managed Payment through eBay™

Navigate the Seller Hub and familiarise yourself with the layout.

"Action is the foundational key to all success"

Pablo Picasso

3

How to List an Item

By now you should have registered on the site you wish to use and have your payment methods set up and ready to go. So, now it's time to sell!

When you first begin to sell online, I would advise you not to lay out too much money initially and instead consider decluttering your home firstly. This will give you the opportunity to investigate as to whether or not selling online is for you. Ideally choose some low cost items that you are happy to list on auction with a 99p starting bid plus your p+p costs.

Start by listing a few items over a 7 day auction. Then, once you have sold a few items you can decide if the 'Buy it now price' is the option you prefer. This is where you state the price you want for the item and the buyer can click to buy it immediately, without having to wait for an auction to finish after a preset number of days.

Step by Step—How to List an Item

Now it's time to choose an item you want to list.

Most websites follow the same format when selling. Firstly, it is extremely important to ensure that the item's title, photos, description and price are correct.

Before you list an item, as I have advised earlier in this book, you will need to have navigated the site you are going to use, get a general 'feel' for the site and note where to find help and policy information.

Before listing I also advise that you read the site's 'Prohibited and restricted items' policy.

OK. Let's get started then!

The following detailed instructions are based on selling an item on eBay™.

Firstly, I would suggest that you search for other examples of the item you are going to list. This gives you the opportunity to see the competition. You will also learn which keywords you could include in your title, and description. And importantly, by researching the item, you will also be able to determine a competitive price.

Click on the 'sell' button or 'create listing' button

You will then be prompted for details of the item you wish to sell. You can use the product ISPN, UPC, ePID, or product name to find the item in the sites catalogue. If the item does not have any of this information don't worry, you can click 'browse categories' and manually find the category under which your item will be listed.

If you were listing a DVD, for example, you would type the title of the DVD or the name of the film in the product name box. The DVD should then be displayed in the search results. It is very important to check the ISPN number matches the DVD you select as there are sometimes different variations of the same film and you need to make sure the one you are selling matches the DVD selected.

If the item you are selling is **not** in the sites catalogue, scroll to the bottom of items shown and click on the box that states, 'continue without selecting a product.' **This will then direct you to the 'create your listing' page.**

The Title Box

The first thing you will be asked for is the title. eBay™ states that, "*A descriptive title helps buyers find your item. State exactly what your item is. Include words that buyers might use to search for your item.*"

Your title needs to stand out, similar to the way in which a newspaper headline grabs your attention. The headline entices you to read on! Most buyers search using mainly keywords to find an item of interest, so it is vital that you include as much information as possible. On eBay™ there are 80 characters available to use in your title. In these 80 characters you should use as many keywords as possible that describe your item. For example, if you are selling an item such as DVD, CD, BLU Ray, or computer game etc., your title should include the following:

The Title Itself

What Format—DVD, CD, Blu Ray, Pc Game, Wii Game, Ps3 Game, etc.

Genre of the Item—Action, Comedy, Family, Thriller, etc.

Actor or Musician Name—State the name of an actor in the film—or musician if selling a CD

Condition—New and sealed, VGC (very good condition), MINT, etc.

For example, If I have the original 'Batman' movie on DVD to list. My title would read:

Batman the movie*DVD*Action*Adam West*original classic family film*NEW*SEALED

The title will then appear in search results if anyone searches using any of the following keywords:

Batman

Movie

DVD

Action film

Family film

Adam West

New

Original film

Classic film

This obviously increases the chances of your item appearing in different searches. People who may not be specifically looking for 'Batman the movie' on DVD but are looking for a 'classic family film' will now see my item. Obviously the more keywords you can fit into your title will increase visibility on the site. Avoid wasting characters—Try not to use words such as 'and,' 'with,' 'or,' or using the same word twice.

Also, do not underestimate the importance of an informative title. Someone once told me they had some items online and were having no luck with sales. Their items were not getting any bids. I offered to have a look at her listings and told her the importance of keywords in the titles. Upon checking her listings, I found that one of the items she was selling was a handbag. Her title read something like this:

'black handbag hardly used'

The handbag was a well-known brand, and it was in mint condition. However, none of this information was in the title or the description box. I offered her some advice on keywords, but it seemed to fall on deaf ears. She probably still has the handbag!

An attention grabbing title should include the following when applicable:

The most common name for the item.

The brand name, artist, actor, designer, author name etc.

If the item is rare or collectable, emphasise this fact. Keywords such as 'rare', 'unique,' and 'collectable,' should all be used if appropriate.

However, do avoid KEYWORD SPAMMING—This is the practice of using irrelevant or misleading words in your title to attract more attention. Only use words that are relevant to your listing! If you need more information regarding this please read the eBay™ policy on Keyword

Spamming. Your listing is at risk of being removed if you include misleading words.

I would also advise you familiarise yourself with these useful abbreviations to use in your title where applicable:

BN—Brand New
BNIB—Brand New in Bag/ Box
BNIP—Brand New in Packaging
BNWT—Brand New with Tags
VGC—Very Good Condition
Mint—As new
OOAK—One of a Kind
OOP—Out of Print
COA—Certificate of Authenticity

The Subtitle Box

The Subtitle box is useful if you need any further space to add to your title. Take note that this has a fee applied to it so if you are going to use the subtitle box make sure it is financially viable. If you are listing a 99p item for example, the subtitle box will wipe out your earning plus more (as the current fee at the time of writing is £2.40.)

Custom Label SKU

The next box is Custom label SKU—This is not always applicable so leave blank if not applicable to your listing.

Category

Double check here that your item is being listed in the correct category. You can list in two different categories.

This will add to your listing fee so make sure it is financially viable to list in two categories. If it is not, select the category that best matches your item.

Variations

You would add variations to your item if, for example, you were listing an item of clothing that you had available in different sizes. Creating multiple variations is not ideal for the beginner and is more likely to be used when you have decided to buy stock and open an online shop. This will not be applicable to any items of which there is only one variety.

EAN Number

eBay™ states this information regarding EAN number . . . *"Buyers often search using product identifiers, so we recommend product identifiers to make sure your listings have maximum visibility in buyer search results."*

If your item does not have an EAN number click on the 'does not apply' option in the drop-down section next to EAN number.

Condition

You will now need to click on the option next to the 'Condition' section. It is very important to select the correct option that describes your item. If you click on 'New' and then send a used item you will be open to a dispute from the buyer as you have not sent the new item they believed they were buying. Do not mislead your buyers with dishonest listings. I would advise you to read the information provided by the site by clicking on the 'i' icon next to 'Condition' to make sure you are following correct policy.

Photographs

This is a very important part of your listing. Invest in a good quality camera as poor quality photos can really affect your sales badly. Make sure you have a clean neutral background for your photos. Taking photos of items against a 'busy' background can take the focus off the item you are trying to sell. You need your item to stand out. Stock photos can be used for some items; however, I would still advise taking your own photo to add to the listing. You may upload up to 12 photos to each listing.

When listing clothing I would advise taking photos from different angles and also if possible display using a mannequin or model.

If you are listing an item such as a board game that is not brand new, upload photos of the contents of the box so the buyer can see that everything is included.

When listing an item where you cannot judge the size of an item consider photographing the item alongside a tape measure so people can gauge the size of the item. You would be surprised how many sellers receive negative feedback stating . . . *"smaller than expected"*

This type of feedback can also be avoided by including more information in the description and also taking a photograph with measurements visible.

When listing an item that has a defect or minor damage etc., include a photograph of the damage. You do not want to mislead the buyer and you must also include this detail in your description. Including this information and photograph shows you are an honest seller.

Please do not use other people's photos. I have had some of my photos from listings copied by other sellers and it just conveys laziness and dishonesty on their part.

When you come to upload your photos onto the listing make sure the photo is the correct way round. Use the rotate button if needed. You will also have the option to crop the picture and also adjust brightness and contrast, sharpen or auto-adjust your photo.

Below the photos you have uploaded you will see an option to . . .

'Display a large photo in search results with Gallery Plus'

Please be aware that there is a fee of £3.00 for this option. Before ticking this option, make sure your item is worth enough to justify the extra fee.

Item Specifics

eBay™ guidelines state this next to the item specifics box . . . "*Provide info about the item you're selling, such as brand, size type, size, colour and style. These details help buyers find your item when they filter their searches and appear at the top of your listing description in a consistent format.*"

I strongly recommend providing as many of these specifics as you can to ensure that your item gets maximum visibility. The item specifics differ depending what category you are selling under. I advise you go through the options of all of the item specifics and choose what applies to your item. If nothing in the drop down list apply to your item, then leave blank.

Item Description

eBay™ guidelines state this about Item description . . . "*Describe the item you're selling and provide complete and accurate details. Use a clear and concise format to ensure your description is mobile-friendly.*

Be sure to include:

Your item's key selling points

Exactly what you're including in the sale. For example, if you're selling used electronics, list which cables it comes with

Full sentences with correct spelling and punctuation throughout"

If your title has attracted a potential buyer to click on your item and learn more, it is your description that finally clinches the deal with a buyer. Your item description needs to be honest and provide a potential buyer with more details/ information about the item.

Always use an accurate, honest description of the condition of the item. State if the item is not brand new and sealed but has never been used. If you are selling a book for example state honestly if it has been 'well read' and indicate if there is any creasing to pages or cover.

When selling an autographed item buyers like to know when the item was signed and how the autograph was acquired. Providing as much information with collectable items is a good selling point.

If the item is a promotional item or Limited Edition make sure to advertise this fact in the description.

IMPORTANT: To repeat for emphasis, when listing any item always make sure you provide an honest description. If the item you are selling has any flaw or defect, mention it.

Selling Details

Auction style—enter your starting bid amount. Make sure you start at a price at which you are happy to sell the item. Starting an item at 99p attracts more potential bidders but there is always a risk that only one person bids and your item then sells for 99p! You can also set a reserve price if you wish. I would advise checking the site's guidelines to learn more about reserve prices.

Fixed Price—I personally prefer the Fixed Price option, where you set the price you are happy to sell the item for instantly. You also have the option to tick the best offer box. This can increase your chances of selling by allowing buyers to negotiate a price with you. You can choose to accept, decline or make a counter-offer.

VAT—Leave this box blank. Visit www.gov.uk for more information regarding if you need to be VAT registered.

Quantity—This is where you enter the amount of this item you have to sell. If you are selling on a Fixed price option and you have one copy of a DVD to sell you would enter 1 in the box, etc. etc.

Private Listing—Tick this box to allow buyers to remain anonymous to other eBay™ members. I always tick this box as I know that a lot of buyers prefer their purchases to remain anonymous to other users checking their feedback.

Make a Donation—To donate to a charity from your sale tick the box. As stated on eBay™ . . . *"eBay for Charity helps you increase your chances of selling by letting you support a non-profit organisation. For your generosity, we give you a fee credit if your item sells."*

Payment Methods—Here is where you will select the option to choose which payment methods you accept.

Return Options—eBay™ states the following . . . *"Most purchases by consumers are protected by the Consumer Contracts Regulations 2013 which give consumer buyers the right to cancel the purchase within 14 days of receiving the item. You are legally obliged to inform consumers about their right of cancellation before the purchase."*

Delivery Details—You will need to provide details of the delivery service you will be using to deliver the item and also the charges for postage and packaging. If you are offering free p+p tick the 'free p+p' box. It is very important to have up-to-date postage rates. I know so many people who have sold something online and have under-estimated the postage charge. Owning some digital scales is also a must!

Know which postage format your item will be when it has been packed:

Letter
Large letter
Small parcel
Medium parcels
Large parcel

I would advise picking up a postage leaflet from your local post office or download a postage chart from www.royal.mail.com

I cannot emphasise enough how important it is to know the maximum sizes and weights allowed for the different formats listed above. It will eat into your profits if you get it wrong!

When selling heavy items, I would advise researching courier services online to compare prices. Visit www.parcelhero.com for more information.

You also have the option to tick to offer local collection. You can then make arrangements with your buyer for a suitable time for collection.

Dispatch Time—Here you will need to choose from the drop down options to indicate when you will dispatch the item. You can choose from 'same working day' to the longest period of 30 days. I will always advise dispatching your item as quickly as possible. Buyers always appreciate a fast dispatch and are more likely to return to your listings. Choose the dispatch time honestly. If you know you cannot offer same day dispatch, then do not offer it. You will be leaving yourself wide open to receiving bad feedback as the item will not arrive as quickly as you have promised.

International Postage—Tick the 'International postage' option if you are happy to post overseas. Always check postage prices carefully before stating your cost. eBay™ currently provide a Global Shipping Programme which means you will post the item to the Global Shipping Programme address within the UK and not incur oversea postage cost.

Read through any other options you have for your listing and complete whichever applies to your item. You can also promote your listing for a small fee which will attract more potential buyers for your item.

Now complete your listing to go live! Good luck!

Once you understand and have familiarised yourself with the listing process, start increasing the number of items you have available for sale. Remember to reply to any enquiries regarding the listed item quickly and politely. You will receive some questions to which you think you have already stated the answer in the item description. You may well be surprised how many people ask questions such as size, measurements etc. when it is already clearly stated in the description. You will also receive some messages that just completely astound you.

I was once selling Ann Summers stockings and received a question from a potential buyer which went something like this . . . ***"Hi, I notice you have size medium and large***

available in these stockings. I was wondering if you would know what size I would need for my husband?"

She then went on to give a rough description of his height and build! I replied that I really couldn't advise what size he would need! He sounded lovely though, I also informed her I would need more information preferably photos of him naked to make a judgement. Of course, I'm joking! I'm just checking you are paying attention!

You really couldn't make it up!

Revising Your Listing

Your listing has now gone live, and you suddenly spot a mistake in your listing. Don't worry, simply click on the listing and click on 'revise your listing' at the top of the page. Then scroll through your listing and make whichever amendments you need to before resubmitting. You may also end your listing if for any reason you no longer wish to sell the item.

Relisting

Unfortunately not all items you list will sell. It is a good idea when relisting your item to consider changing some keywords you have used in your title. Remember your title is your 'Newspaper Headline' enticing people to read on! Maybe the keywords you have used the first time haven't had the desired effect to make people click on your item. You could also add more photographs to your listing. Another important factor is the price. If the item is listed on auction style consider possibly reducing the starting price. If your item is listed on a 'Buy it now' option, you could reduce the price, or tick the 'best offer' option if not already offered.

Tips To Remember

Use your Title to provide as much information as possible using KEYWORDS.

Avoid KEYWORD SPAMMING.

State the condition honestly.

Upload clear photographs and include photographs from different angles if appropriate.

Use a plain neutral background for photographs.

Give a detailed and honest description.

List the item at a competitive price.

State a reasonable P+P price (offer free P+P if you can.)

Revise your listing if you notice any mistakes or have any missing information to add.

"Don't worry if you make mistakes because that's how most people learn."

Alan Sugar

4

How to cancel an order

On some occasions you may need to cancel an order. Always check your messages before preparing items for postage. I have made the mistake of eagerly getting my parcels packed and posted and then read my messages, only to find a cancellation request by a buyer. As the item had already been posted I have had to then request the buyer returns the item (at further expense to myself!) and complete the cancellation process.

Sellers cancelling orders

If a buyer fails to pay for an item and ignores your messages regarding request of payment, you will need to cancel the transaction. You will have been charged a final value fee on the sold item, however, if the buyer fails to pay and you need to relist the item you should not be out of pocket. Opening a cancellation request will result in you, the seller, being refunded your final value fee originally charged to your account. You can then decide if you wish to block the bidder from buying from you again.

Buyers request to cancel order

From time to time you will find that a buyer clicks to buy your item and then realises they have made a mistake.

A common request I receive is *"Can I please cancel this order? My child purchased this without my knowledge!"*

"I purchased the wrong item" and "I have bought the incorrect quantity," are also common mistakes reported.

Always deal with the request promptly and relist your item.

How to cancel an order

Click on your orders in the 'Seller Hub' section of eBay™. There is a drop down list next to your order. There will be a 'Cancel order' option. Click on 'Cancel order.' You will be shown 3 options to choose from regarding the reason for cancellation . . .

'Out of stock or damaged'—Unfortunately from time to time you may find the item you have sold has been damaged or lost. Be honest, cancel the order as soon as you are aware of a problem with the sold item.

'Buyer asked to cancel'—Your buyer has contacted you and requested the cancellation.

'Issue with buyer's delivery address'—If the address on file for you to deliver the item does not seem complete send a message to the buyer asking them to confirm their address. Some buyers fail to respond hence the reason for this cancellation request.

Refund Requests

Your item has been posted but you then receive a message through eBay™ stating that a case has been opened. The policy implemented by eBay™ is to immediately put a hold on your funds until the case is resolved. The most common reason for a refund request is 'Item has not arrived.' Always respond to the case and communicate with your buyer. I will go further into refund requests in the 'Customer Service' chapter.

Return requests

On some occasions your buyer may decide once they have received their item that they no longer want it and wish to return it for a refund.

I recommend reading 'Manage returns, missing items, and refunds for sellers' policy on eBay™ for the most up-to-date information available.

"Productivity and efficiency can be achieved only step by step with sustained hard work, relentless attention to details and insistence on the highest standards of quality and performance."

J.R.T. Tata

5

Preparing your item for Postage

In this section I will provide examples of how to pack your items securely for postage. I would advise having a supply of packaging materials such as:

Envelopes—various sizes

Blank white labels

Clear tape and dispenser

Pens

Cardboard

Boxes

Mailing bags—plastic and padded

Bubble wrap

Packing tape

Scissors

A reliable set of digital scales is also a must!

Most of my family and friends keep their old 'jiffy' envelopes and cardboard etc. for me as they know how much I go through! Even my plumber turned up one day with bags of bubble wrap for me. This all helps to keep costs down, so anytime you can get packaging for free take it, as the more you have to outlay, eats directly into your profits.

Label Printer

As your number of parcels increase I would advise investing in a thermal label printer. Make sure to take into account the cost of labels. A label printer saves you so much time by you not having to write out every address on every parcel. It also looks professional and there is less chance of your item going astray as the address is printed clearly.

Packing Your Item

Once you have successfully sold your item, you now need to prepare it for posting. Always check the item is as you described in your listing. If the item has been damaged somehow send a message to the buyer and be honest. This gives the buyer a chance to cancel their purchase if they wish. Make sure the item is clean and ready to be packed in the best condition possible.

Here are a few examples of items I have sold and how I would pack them:

DVD—Make sure the disc is inserted correctly in the disc holder inside the case. I always put some bubble wrap inside to keep the disc firmly in place during transit. This stops the disc coming loose during transit which would likely scratch the disc. Check there is no damage to the DVD case. If you have a cracked case I would advise you change it before you even list the item for sale, but if you have missed some damage and notice it at point of packing, change the case like for like. You can now either use a bubble padded envelope to post your DVD or a slightly cheaper option is to buy a roll of bubble wrap and cut to size. Wrap the DVD in bubble wrap and place inside a C5 size envelope.

You can post most DVDs as a Large Letter. Please note boxsets etc. will probably have to be posted as a small parcel.

CD—Again, always use bubble wrap to make sure the CD does not come out of the gripper inside the case during transit. I always prefer to pack CDs between two pieces of cardboard taped together and then placed inside a C5 sized envelope taped over to the correct size.

Most CDs may be posted as a Large Letter. Boxsets however will probably need to be posted as a small parcel. If packing two CDs in one package I advise packing them side by side and packed between cardboard this will mean they still fall in the Large Letter category which will be cheaper than if you packed them one on top of the other as this would mean the size of package would be too big for Large Letter and would then be classed as a parcel, which obviously would be more expensive to post.

Greetings Card—You can buy hardboard envelopes which will increase your costs, or you can buy good quality C5 envelopes which are a little sturdier than normal paper envelopes. I would advise you write or place 'Please Do Not Bend' labels on the front on the envelope.

Magazine—When selling magazines, I would advise you to buy the C4 sized hard-backed envelopes. Once you have your envelope taped up with magazine inside I would also place a strip of sellotape around all sides of the envelopes as these are the parts that can get damaged during transit. If the envelope is damaged this can cause the magazine inside to be exposed and damaged. It is also a nice touch to put the magazine inside an A4 sized plastic wallet if it will fit. I would again advise that you write or place 'Please Do Not Bend' labels on the front of the package.

Ornament/ Fragile Item—It is very important to package any fragile items with plenty of bubble wrap etc. If you have the original box and original packaging (such as the polystyrene shaped blocks) use it. If you don't have the original packaging, wrap securely with bubble wrap so it is well protected. You then need to use a suitable sized box for the item. Post Offices do have parcel boxes available for sale however these will increase your packaging costs. I find old shoe boxes are ideal for packaging items. Always keep an eye out for boxes which would help keep your costs down. Always keep empty boxes if you can as you never know when they will be a perfect fit for one of your sales! Place your bubble wrapped item in the box and then fill any spaces with crumpled-up newspaper or bubble wrap. Once you have filled all the spaces tape up the box and give it a gentle shake. If you can hear your item moving around it needs more packaging. For less chance of the box getting damaged during transit your item needs to be tightly secure.

Always affix a 'FRAGILE' label on your package.

Jigsaw/ Toys—If you are selling a used jigsaw puzzle, place all the pieces inside the box, then inside a plastic bag and tape up tightly. I would then either pack the jigsaw box inside bubble wrap and cardboard before wrapping up with brown paper. When packing toys please make sure there are no pieces rattling about as this could cause damage to your item during transit.

Obviously there are lots of different types of items you will sell online. The above is just a small example. The tip to remember is always do the shake test when you have packed your item. If you are going to sell mainly DVDs you might find buying bubble padded envelopes in bulk is your preference in order to save yourself time and effort. It is important to keep packaging costs low but equally importantly, don't scrimp on packaging. Your aim is for the item to get from A to B in perfect condition. If it doesn't arrive perfect for your buyer you will find you will be asked for a refund. You will be out of pocket and possibly receive negative feedback as well.

I once sold a Sexy Santa outfit (brand new and unused I must stress!) and packed it well (or so I thought). But I received a very angry message from the buyer. The packaging had been damaged in the rain and the parcel had ripped open as the postman handed it over. To her dismay her Sexy Santa outfit fell to the floor in full view of her him. She was mortified and angrily informed me I needed to improve my packaging to ensure that if the outer packaging was damaged the item inside was still discreetly packed. She also added she didn't know if she could ever look her postman in the face again. Of course, I felt awful for this lady's embarrassment. I apologised and improved my packaging procedure for items of this nature.

Never take complaints or criticism personally. Always try to learn from that experience and improve your service.

You may also sell items that you do not wish to post. When listing your item please make clear that your item is for collection only and also provide details of the collection timescale you require.

This next comment may seem completely unnecessary to most people, but I must include it. Pack and post the item that you advertised in your listing. A friend who was an artist and was selling some of his paintings online once told me he had been left a negative comment that had really upset him. He had sold a painting to a lady but upon receipt of the painting the lady sent a message stating that her item wasn't as described and left negative feedback. I agreed that the feedback did seem unnecessary and questioned why she would do that. I then jokingly said *"Well, you wouldn't have sent her a different painting would you?"* to which he replied, *"Yes I did, I sent another painting of a similar scene which I felt was the better painting."* I laughed and told him he deserved the negative as he had not delivered the item that was advertised!

Compliment Slips

Compliment slips are a nice gesture, for the purpose of thanking your buyer for their custom. You can also encourage your buyer to contact you with any concerns upon receipt of their item. Unfortunately, parcels can become damaged during transit and sometimes the first you know of a problem is when a refund request has been opened with no communication regarding the problem, or even negative feedback.

I can also recommend including a free gift with an item. When a customer buys a few items from me I usually include a free gift such as a bookmark or free DVD/ CD disc in a paper sleeve. Make sure the inclusion of the free gift does not increase your postage cost. I have received some lovely feedback from buyers regarding my free gifts and it does seem to eliminate a considerable number of items going missing in the post—as well as encouraging repeat custom!

Posting Your Item

Once you have packed your item it's time to get it posted.

I would advise using stamps or print your postage labels online. This helps avoiding long queues at the Post Office. Always send high-value items recorded delivery. Remember to keep all receipts and proof of postage for your records.

Printing Your Own Postage Labels At Home—You can print postage labels through Royal Mail's website and also directly on eBay™. To print directly through eBay™, click on the seller hub section 'orders' and then next to your order click on 'purchase postage label' and follow instructions. Simply print off your postage label and tape onto your parcel.

You then need to pop your post in a post box or parcel box. To find your nearest post box visit www.localpostbox.co.uk. If your item is too big for a postbox search for 'parcel postbox' on www.royalmail.com

If you do not want to print postage labels you can purchase stamp sheets direct from www.royalmail.com

Courier Service—For parcels and heavy items there are a huge range of couriers available. Please visit these websites for further information:

www.parcelcompare.com

www.parcelhero.com

Tips To Remember

Always have a variety of envelope sizes and mailing bags in stock.

Check your messages before posting your item. A buyer may have requested a cancellation or a change of address.

Do the shake test on every item you pack. If it's moving around it is likely to get damaged during transit.

Always double-pack items of a discreet nature. Remember my mortified Sexy Santa Suit customer's embarrassment with her postman!

Use FRAGILE / PLEASE DO NOT BEND labels when needed.

Make sure the address label is written or printed clearly.

Consider printing compliment slips to include with your item.

Find local post boxes or parcel boxes in order to avoid queues at the Post Office (if possible)

"You can't achieve excellence in life if you fear opinion."

Janna Cachola

6

Feedback

Feedback is a very important part of your seller ID. Your feedback number appears next to your ID name and a higher feedback score, gives a buyer an idea of how long you have been selling on the site and if you have a good reputation as a seller. As I write this book I currently have over 91,000 feedbacks. When I first started selling on eBay™, buyers and sellers could leave each other positive, neutral or negative feedback. I actually achieved over 5,000 positive feedbacks before receiving my first negative feedback. I was devastated. I was working so hard and couldn't believe someone could leave me a negative comment without contacting me to make me aware there was a problem. Even though they left me a negative comment I did not want to leave them a negative. I could have left them negative feedback stating ... *"no communication, does not give seller chance to resolve any issues"*

I did contact the buyer but got no reply. Unfortunately, there's not much you can do when this happens. I did know someone who, if they received a negative comment they would then leave the buyer a negative feedback, whilst also sending abusive messages to the buyer! I thought this was basically a case of tit-for-tat which I didn't feel was helpful. Over the years the policy has changed and now sellers cannot leave negative feedback for buyers. This has it's pros and cons. One of the main problems with this is that there is a very small minority of buyers who try to use the feedback system as a form of blackmail.

Blocked Bidder List

On one occasion I had a buyer from overseas who contacted me stating he was interested in buying from me and would be a regular customer. He was interested in my 99p DVDs and stated he would like to buy 10 at a time once a month. I replied and said his custom would be greatly appreciated and I also advised him that I add more stock daily so there should always be new titles for him to look at.

He then contacted me and stated he would only pay a set amount for the postage, for example £5 GBP. I weighed 10 DVDs to get an idea of weight and determined the postage cost to his country using my postage price leaflet. I then contacted him and said that unfortunately I could not post 10 DVDs to his country for that price, as the postage was considerably higher than £5 GBP. He replied that he was TELLING me he would only pay £5 GBP for postage, and I could not charge him a penny more. I said I was really sorry, but I couldn't accept his order. The payment I would be receiving for 10 x 99p DVD's plus postage would leave very little left profit for me. He then got very abusive and said he would click to buy something and leave me negative feedback if I did not agree to the deal. I immediately telephoned eBay™ Customer Care and read out the messages. I was advised to block him from being able to click to buy any of my items. At that time, I was unaware of this facility, but all sellers have a 'Blocked Bidder List' where you can add or remove buyers as and when you need. He was the first buyer I ever blocked, and I wish I could say he was the last but unfortunately he wasn't! I did receive another message from him asking why he couldn't buy anything from me. I told him I had reported him, and he was now blocked from my shop. He immediately apologised, insisted I had misunderstood him, and that he would now pay whatever postage I asked for. I politely told him I was following advice and any further messages he sent me would be forwarded to eBay™ Customer Care. I never heard from him again.

I even received negative feedback from someone on eBay™ when they hadn't even paid for the item. The lady had clicked to buy an item and must have assumed she had paid for it. After a week she left me negative feedback stating, *"Item never arrived, Do not buy from this seller."* I checked the item and found it was still waiting to be paid for. I contacted the lady and asked if she could retract her feedback as I did not feel it was justified. I do not post items out until payment has cleared. She did not even have the decency to respond to my message or retract the feedback. Needless to say, she's now on the Blocked List.

The easiest way to block a bidder is by visiting the overview section of the seller hub. In the section 'Shortcuts' there is a link 'Block bidders'. Click on this link and follow instructions.

Abusive Feedback

I would advise that if you receive abusive or derogatory comments through messages or negative feedback that you never retaliate with abuse.

Remember it is very important to report any messages which you feel are derogatory, abusive or threatening, to Customer Care. There is an option in 'Help and contact' to 'report a problem with a buyer.'

Mostly, if there has been an issue or complaint about an item, the buyer will leave you positive feedback to reflect how quickly you resolved the problem. However, on rare occasions you may find even though you resolve the issue in the buyers favour they will still decide to leave you negative feedback. You have to respect their decision if they feel justified in leaving negative feedback. If the feedback contains a derogatory comment such as name-calling or insinuating you have sold something that is not a genuine product, but you can prove it is a genuine product you can have this feedback removed. You need to follow the instructions for 'revising feedback' in 'help and contact' link. I once received a derogatory comment for a DVD stating that . . . *"looks like it's been stolen, do not buy off this seller"*

I still can't make sense of this comment. How does a DVD look like it's been stolen? I reported this comment, and it was retracted immediately by Customer Care. This was a derogatory comment as it was insinuating I was selling stolen goods! Someone was trying to damage my reputation as a seller.

5 Star Ratings

When buyers leave feedback they can now leave star ratings for:

Item as described

Communication

Dispatch time

Postage and packaging charges

In order to receive top marks for item description make sure your item description includes the condition of the item, size measurements if required, and details of any marks or damage relevant to the item. For example, if you post a book and haven't stated in the item description that there is creasing to the spine, your buyer could rate you a low number of stars for the fact that you have not mentioned any creasing to the spine.

In order to receive top marks for Communication make sure you reply to all messages from your buyer promptly. Buyers also appreciate feedback left for them before they leave a seller feedback. Always communicate politely and ensure you resolve any issues quickly and efficiently.

In order to receive top marks for Dispatch time, I recommend posting your items out within 24 hours of payment received. If someone buys something at 1pm in the afternoon try your best to get the item posted the same day. Buyers do not like waiting longer than the estimated delivery time eBay™ now states on their order. During busy periods such as Christmas or extreme weather conditions delays with delivery can occur. Although this is completely out of the seller's control, sellers often suffer low ratings for delivery times.

In order to receive top marks for Postage and Packaging charges you can offer Free P+P on your listings. This means that buyers cannot rate you for this, you will automatically receive 5 stars. If you want to charge for P+P in order to keep your auction start price low make sure you do not over-charge for postage and packaging. Buyers are not always aware of how much postage and packaging supplies cost so when they see the P+P price they sometimes think it is overcharged. I actually received a message from someone recently stating they wished to cancel their order with me . . . *"Didn't realise the high postage costs, therefore I wish to cancel my order with yourself."*

I was offering free P+P on the item so it's quite worrying when I was selling an item for 99p including free P+P I am accused of charging high postage costs. Luckily if the buyer had purchased it they wouldn't have been able to leave me a low star rating for P+P as it was free!

Neutral Feedback

I personally don't feel neutral feedback is necessary. I have had neutral feedback where the comments have read . . .

"Many thanks"

"No problems"

"Received refund"

"Late arrival.."

"Paid for it to be sent first class and it turned up late"

"Item not as described"

The above statements are not helpful for different reasons.

"Many thanks" infers that the person is happy with their item, and they are offering many thanks to me as the seller,

so why is it neutral? I never found out, as the buyer did not respond to my message.

"No Problems" again infers that the buyer had no problems/ issues with their transaction. Why is it neutral? Again, I never found out as the buyer did not respond to my message.

"Received refund" is not really helpful in describing why a refund was required. It could have been due to being lost in the post or damaged when it arrived. The fact that I refunded the payment shows I resolved the issue in the buyers favour when I was aware of a problem.

"Late arrival" is due to the item being posted later than the buyer anticipated. I post all items out within 24 hours of payment received, Monday to Friday. The service of the postal system is out of a seller's control and the buyer would have seen the postal date mark on the packaging and seen that the item was posted by me, swiftly.

"Paid for it to be sent first class and it turned up late" is not a helpful feedback remark. It is insinuating that I did not post the item out first class. If buyers pay for the first class option I will always post it first class.

"Item not as described" is not a helpful statement without more information. Feedback is left so that other potential buyers can assess the sellers capability. 'Item not as described' could lead some people to think that the buyer is leaving out of their listing any information about damage etc. It could also insinuate a seller is misleading people. I contacted the buyer about the feedback comment, she replied that the DVD I had sent her was not a

boxset that she thought she was buying. The DVD was the same DVD in the photo and the same DVD I listed in the title description. I still don't know to this day why she thought she was buying a boxset.

Negative Feedback

It is very important to avoid receiving negative feedback as this can affect your overall score. If you received 100 positive feedback you will be rated at 100% positive. If you receive one negative feedback out of 100 you would be rated at 99% positive. The higher your score the better chance you have of not having your overall percentage score reduced greatly by one negative feedback.

I am over 91,000 feedback but have scored 2 negative feedback in the past 12 months. My overall score is 100%. I always work with the buyer to avoid negative feedback or have negative feedback revised if possible.

Feedback Revision Request

If you receive negative feedback from a buyer, send them a message. You should always be polite and ask why the negative comment has been left. Make it clear that you are happy to resolve any issues the buyer has and ask them if they would be willing to revise the negative to positive. Usually this works as the buyer is more than happy to revise the feedback to indicate how you have managed to resolve their issue. Unfortunately, there will be times when the buyer is unwilling to communicate with you, hence the reason they leave negative feedback before contacting the seller with their concerns. Don't let a negative feedback put you off selling. I don't like receiving negative feedback; however, I have learnt that you can't please everyone all the time. If it is a deserved negative feedback learn from the criticism and improve where you need to.

To revise feedback, click on the 'Help and contact' link and enter 'Feedback revision request' in the search box. A 'Request a feedback revision' option will appear. Simply follow the instructions on screen.

You can also reply to any feedback comment left for you. By clicking on your feedback score your list of feedback comments will appear. Next to each comment you will have a 'reply' link, simply click on this and type in the comment box what you would like to add.

Leave Feedback Promptly

One thing I have learned about feedback is that buyers do not like to wait for their feedback. Most buyers appreciate feedback as soon as they have paid for their order. Avoid receiving many messages asking *"Can you leave me feedback please?"* by leaving feedback promptly.

I once received a message from a buyer apologising for not leaving me feedback. He had not been well and was going through his order history and was adamant he needed to leave feedback in the order he had purchased. He proceeded to message me giving in depth details of how he was nearly poisoned by a faulty boiler. By the time he had sent me numerous messages detailing his near death experience he could have completed all his feedback! I assured him not to worry about leaving feedback, but he insisted I would receive my feedback when it was my turn!

I never pester anyone for feedback, obviously I am happy to receive positive feedback, so I know the order has been delivered successfully and my customer is satisfied with their purchase.

Tips To Remember

Never threaten a buyer to revise negative feedback—Do not use abusive language.

Always try to resolve the issue your buyer may have and express your apologies for any inconvenience your buyer may have experienced.

Never blackmail a buyer to revise negative feedback—Your buyer can open a case to investigate the transaction. You have no power at all to say if they leave you negative feedback you will not refund them.

Leave Feedback promptly.

"Customers don't expect you to be perfect. They DO expect you to fix things when they go wrong."

Donald Porter

7

Customer Service

When I began selling as a business seller I reached over 5000 feedback before I received my first negative score. I was devastated at the time, but soon realised I had achieved over 5000 happy customers before receiving one negative comment. It is hard not to take a complaint personally, but it is important to strive to work towards resolving the issue by acknowledging the complaint.

Where is My Item?

The most common message you will receive is *'Where is my item?'*

Always reply promptly and politely. For example . . . *'I am sorry to hear your item hasn't arrived yet. I am sure your item will be with you very soon. Can you please confirm your full name and full address so I can look into this? I appreciate your patience and communication. Many thanks.'*

This then gives the customer a chance to reply with the correct postal address. You would be surprised how many people don't update their address and items get delivered to their old address! Sometimes you will not receive a reply. Always send a follow up message to ask if the item has now arrived. Most times it has arrived, but they have forgotten to inform you.

Some sites will state an estimated delivery time on all listings. The best advice I can give is to post your item as soon as you possibly can following receipt of payment. I once sold an item at 11pm one night, and the next morning I had a message from the buyer at 8am asking *"Where is my item?"* I had to laugh at that one!

I would advise you to send any high value items by recorded delivery. Unfortunately, there are a small number of scammers who will purchase items and then open a case stating that the item has not arrived. I would advise you to check your buyers feedback and see if there are any comments left which indicate the buyer has received a refund after an item has been declared lost in the post. Not all of these will be scammers, there are genuine times items do go missing however there could be an issue with the buyers address if there seems to be a few comments regarding lost items in the post.

'The Item has Arrived Damaged'

If a buyer sends you a message and says the item has arrived damaged they will normally attach a photo to show you proof of their complaint. If they have not attached a photo you have every reason to ask to see a photo of the damage or request the item is returned to yourself for examination.

Always aim to resolve the issue as quickly as possible. Most online buyers are polite and happy to communicate with sellers to resolve any issues raised. However, there are some people who can be very rude and threatening. Always answer your messages politely, but in the event of an abusive message always report the buyer through customer services.

Always Try to Resolve the Issue

If your buyer contacts you raising a concern about their purchased item always reply politely and promptly. You may receive a message such as . . . *"my item does not work I want my money back now."*

I would reply to this message politely by saying . . . *"I am sorry to hear you are having a problem with your item. Could you please tell me what is wrong with the item? Why or in what way does it not work? I am always happy to resolve any issues as quickly and efficiently as possible. If a replacement is available would you want a replacement sent out or a refund?"*

If the buyer states that they want a refund you can request they send the item back for testing and issue a refund upon receipt of the returned item. If it is a genuine case you will find your buyer will not have an issue with this. After all, if you returned something back to a shop you don't just walk in and say I've left the item at home, but it doesn't work, and I want my money back now. The shop would request that you return the item to the store for examination before a refund would be issued.

When you reply politely the buyer usually starts replying in a polite manner also. If you think about it if you scowl at someone and shout at them the natural response is to snap back with the same attitude. This just means you both scowl at each other and arguments usually ensue. There's a lady who works at one of our local shops who is so miserable and can be quite sharp with customers. I try to avoid her serving me as she just puts me in a bad mood. One day we were at the self-service tills (which I always end up arguing with!) when the 'seek assistance' red light came on when I put an 'unexpected item' in the bagging area. I still don't understand the 'unexpected item in the bagging area' alert I just scanned it and it's been added to the bill, but the machine doesn't know why I've put it in the bagging area!

The miserable lady arrived shaking her head as if I'd done something wrong. I attempted to explain that I had only tried to put it in the bagging area and the 'lady in the machine went ballistic!' trying to make a joke. She didn't seem to find this funny at all. I then remembered my own advice about always being polite even if I receive a rude or aggressive message from a buyer. I then turned to the lady and said, *"I bet you are sick of these self-service machines."* She then looked at me and smiled, yes, . . . she smiled! It was a look as if to say, 'I hate these machines.' I walked out of the shop that day and thought to myself, 'that lady isn't a bad person, she just hates her job!'

Examples of Customer Complaints

I must stress that I haven't had many bad experiences but the ones I have had are certainly memorable! I once received a message from someone who had bought a trolley 'coin' keyring. The 'coin' is detachable from the keyring, but nevertheless the buyer told me I should be ashamed of myself for selling items that simply did not work. She had tried the trolley coin at 3 different supermarkets, and it would not release the trolley at any of them. The first time she thought it might be a problem with the trolley but after trying to make it work at another 2 supermarkets she informed me the problem was definitely my faulty trolley 'coin' keyrings!

I replied with a polite note saying . . . "*I am very sorry to hear you are having a problem with your item. I personally use one of these trolley coin keyrings and I have never had any issues. I have also sold hundreds of these and have never received one complaint until now. I can only apologise and offer you a full refund for your inconvenience.*"

She replied that I shouldn't sell them anymore as they clearly don't work. She thanked me for the refund but also added that nothing could make up for the embarrassment she felt when people were looking at her not being able to release her trolley. I couldn't understand how it didn't work and as I had sold hundreds I decided I was not going to stop selling them. Something didn't feel right about the entire situation.

A few weeks later I received a message from the lady informing me that she needed to apologise. She felt awful and wanted to pay her money back. Her item was not faulty after all, and she even admitted that she did not know she had to unclip the coin from the keyring to insert into the trolley! No wonder she had a crowd of people staring at her trying to insert a trolley coin into the trolley still attached to her keyring! It is surprising though that no-one thought to show her it needed to be unclipped from the keyring first. When I finished laughing I thanked her for being so honest.

I have received some very strange messages over the years. Sometimes I have even been completely baffled by them.

This is a message I received recently (bad spelling included) . . .

"Dear Sir / Madame.

After checking my bank, I can see you have failed in your offer of a full refund.

I can only question your company and its procedures that they do not take customer care and satisfaction seriouserly.

Why go through all this letter writing, and stress again and again for such a small amount?

Is your company fraudulent, is it run by crooks?

Why not issue the refund just for customer relations, I'm fed up with your terrible customer care.

I am starting to believe you are not a real company, but infact fraudulent.

I will be going through a case on eBay for full refund, and I will be contacting trading standards. To push through a case for poor trading standards.

And for fraudulent trading practices, as it's clear there is something very suspect going on in your company.

I have sent multiply letters, with no refund, and very substandard customer care.

Also, I shall be placing a link on social media showing and shaming this obvious scam.

To say I am fed up and disappointed in you is an understatement

Yours angerally, Mrs Joy

I have to assume this was a joke message sent, simply from the 'Yours angerally, Mrs Joy.' How ironic! Anger and Joy do not go together! I do not know the reason for these messages, but I do believe there are some very bored people with too much time on their hands. I did reply out of courtesy simply asking, 'What Item did you purchase from me?' But as you can probably guess I never received a reply.

During the Coronavirus 2020 when postal services were disrupted and delayed in some areas of the country due to staff shortages, I received this message . . .

"Well item still not arrived. Going to give it till Fri, then if item has not arrived I want a refund. Don't blame covid 19 for postal as the postal is working fine and has been fine for all other items that I have ordered over the last two months. But it seems really difficult to get a small piece of card from you. Really hope it's here by Fri, as I want to give good feedback."

I replied to this message and stated that there was still delays in the UK however I was sure the item was on its way and should hopefully arrive soon. Then I received this message . . . *"Well today is Friday and your small piece of card never arrived, my guess is that royal mail have never or ever have had eny experience of delivering things made from paper or card. I bet you blame them. Funny how all other stuff I have ordered over the last few months from reliable ebay sellers turned up. refund me it's the least you can do today."*

The messages have been copied and pasted as they were sent to me, so any spelling mistakes are from the original messages. Note that the messages never start off with 'Hi,' or end with a farewell. The buyer seems to not want to believe that the postal service could ever mislay a parcel.

Their conclusion is that I never posted the item in the first place! I forwarded this message to customer services for investigation as I find comments like these defamatory, and I don't think sellers should have to put up with abusive messages. If all sellers do this, then these online users can be investigated to see if they are sending abusive messages to other sellers. This is a form of trolling I believe which should not be allowed.

I also received this complaint recently from someone who had not bought anything from me but had issues with the DVDs I was selling. I have copied the full conversation below (my replies are in bold) . . .

Your DVD's are all advertised as GENUINE

The pictures that you show in lots of your ads are clearly not genuine dvd's.

I sell enough DVD's to pick out dodgy ones a mile off

See below what this Dvd should look like (not with the edges missing like yours)

Be interesting to hear your response.

Do most customers even know the difference?

Hi

I do not sell copies at all. I will be forwarding your message to customer services for investigation. I consider your comments defamatory and will seek their advice. I only sell genuine DVDs and CDs etc.

The pictures of the disc's on many of your dvd listings are definitely not genuine dvd releases.

You are welcome to forward any messages and seek any advice regarding my comments if you think I'm trying to damage your good reputation.

Hi

All the discs I have listed are genuine. I have discarded the original covers and cases. As I cannot compete with other sellers selling the same titles, sometimes I have to just sell the discs by themselves as it is cheaper to post. I appreciate your comments however I can assure you I do not sell copies. I have been an online seller for many years and am proud of my reputation. I would not risk my reputation to sell copied DVDs.

Hello,

I feel your pain when it comes to trying to compete with other sellers.

There is nothing wrong with discarding the cases and covers to save a little on postage costs. You do have a good reputation with 90,000+ feedback that you must be proud of.

I used to own a movie rental store years ago and have also been a market trader so I do know what I'm talking about!

I'm not sure if selling movies is your main source of feedback, I'm guessing not.

Did you see the difference between the picture I sent you and the disc that you are selling? To the trained eye, it's completely different. Most of these 99p disc's that you are selling are different to the ones that I sell.

Selling these for 99p doesn't make you any money, it just adds to your feedback.

Most of my feedback is from sale of DVDs etc. I wish you well with your sales in the future. I have been a DVD seller for many years and I maintain that I do not sell copies. There are many different disc pictures for the same film as there are different DVD editions of the same films. I appreciate your comments.

I still beg to differ.

I'm not stupid and I clearly understand everything there is to know regarding different pictures and editions of the same movie.

Lots of your disc's are so badly printed that the complete title doesn't even fit on the disc.

Example 1: Days Of Glory (has the D and the Y missing)

Example 2: The It Crowd (has the T and the D missing)

There are so many examples of similar errors in your listings and you are clearly telling me that these are GENUINE

They don't even have the copyright warnings around the outside edge of the disc's . . . funny that hey!

Where it says . . . Unauthorised copying, hiring, lending, public performance, radio or Tv broadcasting of this Dvd is prohibited.

How can you claim that these are official genuine releases when clearly they are NOT ?

Hi

The discs are inside paper sleeves to protect them that's why you can't see the whole of the disc picture.

If that's the case and they are in white sleeves please accept my apology.

I Feel bad now ☹

Hi

Apology accepted. I was wondering what you meant about the edge of the discs etc. I will make it clearer in new listings that the discs are inside paper sleeves. The reason for this is to protect them from getting scratched.

The reason I include this conversation is to show how to respond to a message politely. The first message is a direct accusation against me inferring that I am not selling genuine DVDs. I did not have a clue what the basis of the accusation was. However as we continued communicating it became clear. The person sending me the messages was also a seller on the same site. I had a look at his listings and saw that he was selling DVD discs in clear plastic sleeves where you can see the whole of the picture on the disc. In my photos my discs are photographed inside white paper sleeves which means the whole picture on the disc was not visible. Rather than be abusive and defensive I ended my communication on a positive note.

Always improve your listings when prompted by a query. Some things may appear obvious to most people but not always to everybody. Remember the lady with the trolley coin keyring! I would never think I would need to state in my listing that the trolley coin needed to be detached from the keyring as I assumed everybody knew this!

I must stress I do not receive many complaints. I have had the occasional message correcting a mistake I have made in a listing. I always thank the person who brought the mistake to my attention.

Abusive and rude messages are very rare. I immediately block any buyer who sends abusive material. I know so many people who have quit selling online due to not being able to deal with some buyers messages/ feedback. Learn and improve from bad experiences. I recommend visiting the eBay™ Community page. There is a discussion page available for 'Member to Member support' to which every buyer and seller can refer. It is a lovely community to be part of and other users are so helpful.

Even though this chapter is about dealing with Customer complaints I must also add that the majority of my customers send messages to thank me for my good service. I also have regular customers who send me messages just to say hello and wish me continued success with my eBay™ shop.

I receive numerous messages thanking me for making the item available for sale in the first place! Some people share memories and reasons they have purchased the item. I remember selling some True Crime Magazines in the past. One lady, from America, wanted to know how many different magazines or books I had available about a particular serial killer. I responded and put together a package which she was happy to purchase. A few weeks later she asked again if I had anymore magazines and books about this serial killer. I replied I had sent her everything I had available. I was intrigued at this point as there was something about this request that seemed strange. She thanked me and must have felt she needed to explain why she was so interested in this serial killer. It turned out that she had been an intended victim but had managed to escape. She was in the process of writing a book about this traumatic event in her life and wanted to learn more about the history of this serial killer.

I also received another message regarding a True Crime Magazine I sold. The buyer sent me a message confirming that the magazine had arrived safely. He then added the reason he had purchased the magazine. It turned out that the murderer featured in the magazine had once lodged at his house. *"Of course"* he added, *"We didn't know he was capable of such crimes if we did he would never have been allowed in our house!"*

A lovely man once got in touch to ask if I wanted his collection of War Machine Magazines. He had noticed I was selling some. He had some in his loft and offered them to me for nothing, all I had to do was cover the postage costs. I thanked him very much and agreed to send him money for the postage. He said he would be back in touch when he got the magazines out of the loft and packed them for me. I didn't hear from him for a while and forgot all about the magazines. A few weeks later he got in touch and apologised for the delay, he had fallen out of the loft while retrieving the magazines! He felt awful for keeping me waiting . . . and I felt bad that he had fallen out of the loft! He stills keeps in touch and regularly sends me messages to ask how I'm doing.

I must also include this very funny experience. I always follow the correct procedures while selling online and never list anything that knowingly violates a policy in place, so imagine my surprise, following a sale I made online, to find two policemen knocking on my door late at night.

The first thought entering your mind when you answer the door to the police is, *Has there been an accident?*

One of the policeman immediately set my mind at rest and stated *"Please don't worry we are not here to report bad news. There's nothing to worry about, you are not in trouble."*

I asked what was wrong and he then asked me, *"Have you sold anything online recently?"*

I laughed and replied that I have sold many things online and explained I was a full-time online seller. Could I tell them what I sold he asked? It was far easier to show them, so I invited them in and proceeded to switch the laptop on. Obviously, at this point I am racking my brain thinking what could I have possibly sold that results in the police turning up on my doorstep!

They couldn't reveal all the details of the 'crime' as it was under investigation. When I showed them my online shop they realised, as I sold so many different lines of stock, that they would need to give me more information. One of my lines was plastic wallet cards which people buy as gifts. These cards have lovely sentimental messages. One of the cards had the message *"I'm sorry"* and then a lovely verse included. It turned out that I had been used to harass someone! A woman living in Scotland had received one of my 'I'm sorry' keepsakes and immediately assumed it had been sent to her by an ex-boyfriend, whom she had a restraining order imposed upon. He had broken the restraining order by making contact with her although technically he had not made direct contact as he used me to deliver the message!

They had traced me as my return address was on the reverse of her package, so I then had to make a statement informing police that I had not knowingly been part of the harassment! I was also told I may need to attend court in Scotland, and I replied that was fine if they were paying for my expenses!

The police left and said they would be in touch. I excitedly told Gary that I had a trip to Scotland planned for us! Then, a few weeks later I received a phone call from a policeman in Scotland. I was asked to go over my statement with him, which I did but at the end of the call he informed me that I would not be required to attend court to testify after all. I then had to inform Gary our trip was off! This has to be the most bizarre experience of my online selling life!

Tips To Remember

Always reply promptly and politely.

Aim to resolve any issues as quickly as possible.

Seek advice from Customer Care when needed.

Learn from criticism to improve your service.

"Seek out opportunity and seize it."

Deborah Meadon

8

Researching Stock

After building some seller's experience it is now time to look for stock. Build-up stock at a manageable level for you. Set a sensible and reasonable budget for stock. If you are still getting a feel for it, start by looking around charity shops and car boot sales for bargains.

Deciding What to Sell

You now need to do some research and see what stock you want to sell. There are many categories to look at while researching. Again, spend some time navigating the site you are going to use and see which categories are available. I have included a list of current categories available on eBay™ in the final chapter of this book.

The obvious golden rule when buying stock is buy at the cheapest price you can. However, this does not mean buy cheap or inferior quality goods. I once bought some money belts (brand new and sealed stock) at a good price and was making a good profit. The problem was that as it turned out, they were very poor quality. The zips would break after a couple of uses. I only found this out when I received complaints and demands for refunds. Needless to say, these stock items ended up making me a loss as there was also the postage costs etc. to take into account. This could have been avoided if I had opened the item and inspected the goods properly. If you have the chance to buy a job lot of new stock always open one and inspect it! You do not want to sell poor quality items.

I would advise selling items you are familiar with or have a general interest in. I started by selling DVDs as I am a huge movie fan and found it a very easy category to list in. By selling DVDs when I receive queries regarding a film I can normally answer these queries from my knowledge of the movie. Of course, some questions take you by surprise. I was once asked this question regarding a DVD I had listed . . . *"I see this film has Aaron Eckhart in it. Can you let me know how many minutes in total Aaron is actually on screen through the whole movie?"*

This is the kind of question which I find is an unreasonable request. Answering a question like this will take up too much of a seller's time to make the sale worthwhile.

I always try to have a variety of stock in my shop. This attracts a wide range of buyers. Buyers of DVDs normally only buy a couple of them, however by having other lines such as greeting cards you will get buyers who browse your other items and could end up buying other items that they were not originally looking for.

If the price is right don't be afraid to take a gamble. I once spotted a box of wrestling magazines at a car boot sale. I had never sold wrestling magazines before however, the seller offered me the whole box for £5. I remember thinking I might make £1 per magazine so bought them. I started selling them on auction from 99p starting bid. I ended up making between £5 and £10 per magazine. It turned out that some wrestling magazines are rare and collectable but as I am not a wrestling fan I didn't have a clue as to the value of these magazines. When I have surprise successes like this I refer to it as 'a Del Boy Moment.'

As your experience of buying and selling grows you will soon develop an eye for bargains! Here are some examples of items to stock and what to look out for when buying them:

Clothing

I have sold only a few items of clothing online and tend to stick to brand new items with tags still attached. Used clothing can often have signs of wear. Always complete a thorough examination when buying.

I would also recommend that if you are going to sell clothes on a regular basis think about investing in a mannequin. Displaying your garments this way helps make your photos really stand out and show the clothing to its full potential.

Books

Always try to buy books that are brand new or look brand new. Have up-to-date knowledge of popular authors and new releases. Sometimes you can spot a newly released book in a charity shop or car boot sale. Books do sell well on eBay™, however please be aware of postage costs as most books will have to be posted as a small parcel. I find books tend to sell better in small lots rather than individually as this saves on postage. Check the condition of the book carefully—some buyers do not appreciate it when pages have been turned over in the corner. It seems a silly thing to say but always check all pages are intact and the book is complete!

If you have a love for books why not look into rare titles. I know someone you bought a book at a charity shop for 50p and sold it online for over £1,000! He knew what he was looking for as he was a dedicated book seller, but even he was surprised when he made that much money!

Games/ Jigsaws

Some board games are highly collectable and can fetch high prices online.

When buying a second-hand game check all the contents are there—I have bought some games and arrived home only to find that half the contents are missing, after being told by the seller (normally car boot sales) *"everything's there, it's hardly been used."* I know it sounds bad but never take the sellers word for it. Always check the contents and condition before you part with your money. If you do buy a game with some of the contents missing don't despair. Sell off the parts you do have as people often lose parts of board games and need to replace the odd component. Some figures from board games can often go for good money!

Ideally buy games and Jigsaws which are brand new and sealed—Avoid used jigsaws. It's a tedious task counting all the jigsaw pieces to check all 1000 pieces are there! Think of how many items you could have listed on eBay™ in the amount of time it takes to count all those jigsaw pieces! Unless you like doing jigsaws and then you can take a photo of the jigsaw complete for your listing.

Brand new and sealed board games and jigsaws are very good sellers especially near Christmas. Special editions of classic games are also collectable.

You can often pickup brand new games and jigsaws at car boot sales and charity shops for around £2 each. It's always worth a gamble in my opinion, you will nearly always get your money back at the worst and at best make a tidy profit. I once sold a Donald Trump game picked up at a car boot sale for £1 and sold it on for £35.

DVDs

DVDs are still a good seller online even in this age of downloads. Top tips for buying DVDs for resale . . .

Always check the cover for damage—Sticker marks and rips or tears can decrease the value of the DVD. The case can always be changed but the cover should be in pristine condition.

Take the disc out of the disc tray and examine the disc for marks, scratches—Avoid any discs with deep scratches at all costs. When browsing in charity shops you would be surprised to find how many damaged discs there are.

If the disc has some minor surface marks, which is quite common, these can easily be cleaned up and repaired with Vaseline or peanut butter.

You could also invest in a disc repair machine but make sure you are aware of the costs of cleaning products required for these machines. The JFJ Easy Pro Disc Repair Machine is one of the best currently on the market.

Check it is a genuine DVD—There are also a lot of copies for sale in charity shops. This is not the charity shop's fault as some of the copies are really close to the real thing. As I have dealt in DVD sales for many years now I am pretty good at spotting copies. Avoid buying or selling copies of any kind. Copied discs are normally quite easy to spot as they will have coloured labels applied to the disc instead of the picture directly printed onto the disc.

CDs

Exactly the same advice applies to buying and selling CDs—as with DVDs. However, with CDs you also need to check the CD case and sleeve inlays as they are often damaged when buying second hand. Serious collectors of CDs like to know the condition of the disc, the inlay and the case.

Magazines/ Comics

Some Magazine issues and comics are highly collectable.

When buying magazines check for signs of damage such as creasing, tears, or writing on the cover. Check all pages are complete and intact. Magazine buyers are often collectors who do not want to buy damaged magazines/ comics etc.

Used magazines that have been originally hand-delivered by a newsagent can often have the surname of the original buyer written somewhere on the front cover. This doesn't seem to put people off buying however you must always include this detail in your description.

If you buy a magazine on a regular basis for yourself why not keep them for a while and then sell either individually or in a bulk lot to recoup some of your money? You may be pleasantly surprised how collectable some magazines are. Especially overseas.

Video Games And Consoles

There are so many different types of video consoles. I can't keep up with them all! Over the years I have sold so many different games and consoles.

Some games require codes and cannot be re-used. Make sure you do your research when buying games. Some codes unlock parts of a game. If I am selling a used computer game I always state that the item is used and cannot guarantee if there is a code.

With all games check the disc is not scratched, and that the instruction booklet is included. Games still sell without the instruction booklets, but this will normally affect the re-sale value.

When buying consoles check that all the bits are there. Always check the remote control's battery pack as a common problem with anything that needs batteries is damage by leaking batteries.

I often buy Wii job lots which include the console and a number of games. You get very little for the console now, however, some of the Wii games can still fetch high prices.

Ornaments

Ornaments with their original box are usually worth more money than an unboxed ornament.

If an item is a limited edition there is sometimes a certificate included. Your item could be slightly de-valued without the certificate.

If you are considering buying ornaments or fragile items to sell, please scrutinise the item before buying. Look for any sign of damage or repair. Even a small hairline crack can de-value the item greatly.

I remember seeing a lovely Red Indian ornament at a market. I spent a good ten minutes scrutinising it, and couldn't find anything wrong with it all. The seller wanted £10 for it. I thought I'd got a bargain! Walking back to the car I noticed the arm had been broken at the elbow and glued back on. I had a *"should've gone to Specsavers"* moment because I don't know how I missed it. It was really badly repaired. I ended up keeping the ornament and wrapped a piece of white material round it so it looked like the Red Indian had a war wound!

Electronics

When buying electronics to sell on, make sure you test the item at time of purchase. Take time to carefully inspect the item. If the item also takes batteries, check the part of the item where the batteries are inserted. If a battery has leaked then the item may be ruined.

Vinyl Records

Vinyl has recently made a comeback. There seems to be a love of most things retro now so if you can spot a bargain, buy it. Used vinyl records are often scratched so when buying at car boot sales or purchasing job lots please check the condition of the record. Vinyl records are also used for making novelty gifts such as clocks, framed disc displays, and bowls. Do some research into this area as there is good demand for vinyl records at the moment.

VHS Tapes

Another retro item making a come-back is the good old VHS tape. I used to love going to my local VHS movie rental store when I was younger. When DVDs came out most people replaced their VHS collection and threw their tapes out. Well, now it seems they are back in fashion! Some films that were not issued on DVD are now worth a lot of money on VHS. The problem with re-selling old VHS tapes is that unless you watch every VHS tape before you list it, you won't know if there are any parts of the film where the actual tape has been damaged. VHS tapes however can be recycled. There are some lovely novelty ideas. My own favourite is VHS tapes being turned into a LED night light. They look fantastic—have a look on eBay™!

Collectables

Art, coins, antiques etc. are also very good sellers online. Always inspect your item carefully for any signs of damage that could de-value it in any way. When buying collectable items do your research and stick to your budget—don't forget you need to make a profit! When buying autographed memorabilia always buy from a reputable seller. There are so many fakes out there, and if you are going to deal in autographs you need to really do your research.

I have made novelty gifts using old coins in the past. Pre-decimal sixpences are very popular as many people make 'lucky sixpence' gifts using old sixpence pieces. Some people use the coin's year of issue to make a novelty gift for someone born in the same year, for example.

I have a very popular line selling lucky sixpences. I used to have a regular buyer who would message me and ask for 100 at a time. It turned out he lived locally so I made a deal with him for a regular order. He invited me to his apartment. It turned out he dealt in gold and silver coins and my lucky sixpences were a free gift he was sending to his customers with their orders. It also turned out he was a magician and mentalist. I took my mother with me one day and he ended up doing a free magic show for us! He also gave my nephew, Ethan, a small gold bar one day which made his day, he felt like a millionaire!

But whatever you choose to sell, remember my top tip:

If the item is £1 or less and looks in good condition it's worth a gamble!

Tips To Remember

Research categories available and the most popular selling categories.

Make a list of rare items currently selling online. Remember my book seller friend's huge profit. Paying 50p for a rare book and selling it for over £1000!

Always inspect the condition carefully.

When buying high-value items always buy from a reputable seller.

Research retro and novelty ideas.

Set a budget to invest in stock.

"We've got some
Half price cracked ice
And miles and miles of
carpet tiles
TVs
Deep freeze
And David Bowie LPs.
Ball games
Gold chains,
What's-names
Pictures frames
And leather goods
And Trevor Francis track suits."

Lyrics from the 'Only Fools and Horses' theme song, by John Sullivan

9

Sourcing Stock

Research done and it's now time to buy some stock for resale. One of the most common questions I get asked about selling online is . . .

"Where do you get your stock from?"

The simple answer is 'everywhere!' I do not have one source. There are so many places to buy stock and here are examples of the main sources I use.

Car Boot Sales

I love visiting a car boot sale. You can find some fantastic bargains. To locate a car boot sale near you do simply do an internet search. I have found the following sites helpful:

www.carbootsales.org

www.ukcarboot.co.uk

www.nobles-promotions.co.uk

www.carbootjunction.com

Top Tips For Buying at a Car Boot Sale

Take a shopping trolley if you can, this will make it so much easier than carrying bags.

Get there early—'The early bird catches the worm.' Please note that some car boot sales charge a higher entrance fee for early entrance.

Take plenty of change. Offering the correct change helps the seller out and also looks better for you if you have managed to haggle. If a seller wanted £5 for an item and you barter down to £3, I think it looks bad if you offer them a five pound note.

Inspect the item and never take the sellers word for it. The number of times I have bought a DVD at a car boot sale having been told there was no need to check the contents as the disc is perfect. And then upon checking the DVD at home I have found the discs scratched and in some cases no disc included at all! So don't feel bad for checking the item to make sure it meets your satisfaction.

If you are interested in a few items on a particular stall, try to negotiate a deal with the seller for a discounted price if you buy more than one item.

Go round the stalls at the end of the selling day when sellers are packing away. Some sellers go straight to the tip after a car boot sale and throw the unsold items away as they only wanted to have a clear out. This is your chance to make a seller an offer for their unsold items. I have bagged many bargains this way!

For more tips on car boot buying search www.youtube.com for 'car boot haul.'

Markets

The following websites are useful to find markets near you . . .

www.theculturetrip.com

www.information-britain.co.uk

www.visitengland.com

Over the years I have become a regular at our local markets and got to know quite a few of the market traders. I met a lovely couple Michael and Sue, who have been regulars on the North East Markets for years. They used to have a stall every weekend at the popular Tynemouth Station market.

I used to go to markets before I started selling on eBay™ with my mother. I would hear Michael talking to his customers and I would say to my mother *"Doesn't he have a lovely voice?"* and she would agree. He was lovely and always so enthusiastic with his customers. Over the years I got to know them well, so after registering self-employed as a sole trader, I approached Michael and asked if had any stock he wanted to sell off.

We have become good friends over the years. Michael and Sue are two of the nicest people I have ever met and have offered me some wonderful lines of stock over the years.

When they see me approaching their stall now they say *"Eeh, it's eBay Dawn"*. Michael nearly always says when I see him *"I was just thinking of you"* then tells me which lines he had in mind for me. *"I think this will be a winner for you, Dawn"* is one of his favourite lines! He also likes his puns! He was trying to sell some kites to me one day . . . *"These will fly out, Dawn!"* was his sales patter! Whatever stock I buy from Michael he is always happy to know if I have done well with it.

You would be surprised how many market traders are happy to sell off some of their stock off in bulk. After getting to know Michael and Sue, other market traders would call me over to their stalls to see if I wanted to know what deals they could do for me!

I remember meeting Brian, a market trader at Tynemouth Station. He shouted over *"Are you eBay Dawn?"* "Yes" I replied. He then proceeded to point out stock he was happy to sell off cheaply. He has also became a regular supplier over the years.

I also have other suppliers from the markets who regularly get in touch with offers of stock. Buying in bulk puts some people off due to not having space to store the stock or worrying about how long it will take to sell it all. If you are getting a bulk lot at a really good price, you can always split these into smaller lots and sell on that way.

Shop Sales

You can also source stock at shops that are closing down or selling off stock to clear old lines. Most shops have a clearance corner or bargain bin. In the early days of selling, I used to buy most of my stock from shops and knew where all the clearance sections were. I remember buying some DVDs from a bargain bin one day. One of the titles was the story of a stunt driver. I looked up the title online and found it was rare and listed it at a competitive price. The DVD sold quickly and upon checking the order details to post the item out found the name of the buyer was the same as the stunt driver featured in the DVD. The next week the same buyer contacted me and asked if I had any more copies of the DVD he had purchased. During the week I had already been back to the bargain bin and bought the other copies as I had realised it was rare. I informed him of how many copies I had available, and he agreed to purchase them. Curiosity had got the better of me and I sent him a message asking if he was the stunt driver featured in the DVD. He confirmed he was the World Record Holding Stunt Driver in question. I was thrilled at this, I offered him discount in return for a signed picture of him. The following week I received a signed poster from him which I still treasure!

Auctions

Auction houses are also a good way to buy stock and an exciting day out if you like the experience of buying at auction. Always find out what fees the auction house apply to the final price before bidding though, as you could receive a bigger bill than expected!

To find your local auction house have a look at the following websites . . .

www.police-auctions.org.uk

www.the-saleroom.com

www.auctionfinder.co.uk

www.auctionsalefinder.co.uk

Auction houses normally have a day set aside before the actual sale day where you can view the items available. This gives you time to inspect the item, and research possible selling prices. Have in mind the maximum price you are willing to bid and try to avoid getting carried away and end up paying more than you wanted to. You will also be charged a fee on top of the bid price offered. Make sure of all extra costs/ fees before making your bid.

At some auction houses you can also ask to see a list of unsold lots and make an offer. I did this on one occasion when I went to a local auction house after the sale, with a friend. My friend said there was a huge box full of books which he thought would interest me that I could probably get them for a cheeky offer of £5! He offered the price of £5 to the manager of the auction house, who then checked his paperwork and agreed to the price.

After going through the books at home, I immediately put a collection together to sell on to a book seller I knew. By the end of that same day, I had made a good profit on my purchase and still had half of the books left to sell. The next day my friend contacted me and said "*I'm really sorry Dawn, but the manager of the auction has been in touch, and he shouldn't have sold the books at that price. He wants them back!*" I replied I'd already sold half of them! But my friend had a history of playing jokes on people so I thought he must be winding me up! Surely a manager of an auction house couldn't be that incompetent!

I thought no more of the incident until a few weeks later when I visited the auction house again. The manager recognised me and approached me. "*That was a really dirty trick you did, not bringing those books back.*" I was taken aback at how unprofessional he was. I never found out the full story but basically his incompetence was to blame for the whole thing. He should have had a note in his paperwork as to whether the seller of the books had set a reserve price. I replied that by the time I received the message I had already sold half of the books. He replied, *"You're not that good!"* 'Oh, but I am,' I thought to myself!!

I later witnessed the same manager having to apologise to a potential buyer for not putting his bid forward during the auction. I will not name the auction house, but it has a very deserved poor reputation and needless to say I doubt I will ever go there again!

Cash and Carry

There are many Cash and Carry outlets available. Some Cash and Carry outlets allow you to place orders online and offer fast delivery to your chosen address.

Here are some websites you may find of interest . . .

www.crosswear.co.uk

www.poundwholesale.co.uk

www.evanscashandcarry.co.uk

www.joneswholesale.com

I used to visit two local Cash and Carry outlets and found the staff to be friendly and helpful. Due to COVID restrictions with the many confusing guidelines that kept changing every day, an appointment was required to visit the store. I found this was detrimental to my business as I was having to wait for available appointments rather than nip into the store whenever I needed. I found some online Cash and Carry businesses online and found I could order the same stock for roughly the same price with free next day delivery! This saved me so much time by not having to travel to the store.

Online ordering is so much easier and most online suppliers provide next day delivery.

Once you have established the type of stock you wish to sell, use an internet search to find Cash and Carry outlets which match your needs. For example, if you want to sell greeting cards search for 'greeting cards cash and carry.'

You can also click on 'list of wholesale suppliers' on eBay™ for prices ranging from only 99p.

Online Selling Sites

Sourcing stock online is also a productive way to build up your stock. When looking at a potential job lot to purchase, take a good look at the list of items included. Work out how much you are likely to make by selling the items individually. Always take in to account fees and postage costs when working out your potential profit and then calculate what your maximum bid will be.

I personally prefer to buy job lots on a 'buy it now' price instead of auction. The main reason for this is you know the final price immediately, and you know the seller is getting the price they are happy with as they have set the 'buy it now' price. I have had experience of buying on auction in the past and then because the seller hasn't got the price they wanted they cancelled the order after the auction finished. So, it is therefore possible that you might have wasted a week waiting for that particular job lot and not bid on other listings due to limited finance for stock purchases.

Use keywords when looking for job lots, such as . . .

Lot

Bundle

Collection

Job lot

Wholesale lot

Joblot

Clearance Sale

Pallet job lot

It is also possible to pick up some great bargains on www.gumtree.com. I love Gumtree™ and often look there for personal and business use. I have purchased some great bargains over the years. Enter your postcode to find items for sale in your local area.

www.shpock.com—Shpock is an online marketplace similar to Gumtree™. I have personally only used Shpock once and ended up with the most priceless bargain I could ever wish for, my cat Pixie! She was advertised on Shpock for only £10. A gorgeous tabby pictured, alongside her two brothers, aged only six weeks old. I fell in love the moment I saw her. Financially she costs us a small fortune as she is a very picky eater but the pleasure she brings us more than makes up for this!

www.facebook/marketplace—Another useful way to pick up bargains!

You would also be surprised how many people are happy to give items away, especially when moving home. I would personally recommend free sites for picking up items of furniture, office equipment etc., which you are going to buy for personal use. I once replied to an ad on Gumtree™

offering the full contents of their shed for free if collected same day. I arranged to collect asap. Upon arriving they had the contents of the shed on the drive ready for us to take away. I was informed that some of the contents were damaged goods and would need to be thrown away but also that some of the items may be worth something. I asked if they were sure they didn't want anything, and the man replied that I would be doing him a favour as he knew I would need to dispose of the rubbish which would mean a trip to the skip!

Two trips later we had the contents of the shed in our garage. More than half of it had to be thrown away but amongst the boxes was a full set of encyclopedias. The man had mentioned them and said, *"they could be worth a few quid for you."* He wasn't wrong! After a few months of advertising them I finally sold them for £100!

Sites such as 'freecycle', 'freegle' and 'olio' are also ideal for picking up packaging for free!

Opportunities to buy stock can arise at any time. I once asked my mother if she wanted to meet the comedienne Sarah Millican who was signing copies of her new DVD at a local supermarket. I was a fan and wanted her new DVD anyway, so I was really happy that I was going to meet her and have my DVD signed. The 'Del Boy' came out in me while standing in the queue though. My mother wasn't bothered about getting a DVD signed so I asked her to get one signed for me to sell on eBay™. I didn't want it personalised as that would de-value it. When you sell autographed items it pays to not have the item personalised. Most collectors prefer the item with the autograph only.

So, we approached Sarah and she signed my DVD. 'To Dawn' I manage to stutter to her, and she was really friendly and funny. My mother then passed her DVD to sign, and Sarah asked her, *"who do I dedicate it to?"* Mother, quick as a flash, replied *"to the highest bidder."* Sarah laughed and made a joke of her own, *"you'll only get about £1.50 for it!"*. Mother replied that the DVD was going to be given as a gift to someone but doesn't yet know who, so could she just sign her name? So, Sarah signed *"Merry Xmas, love Sarah Millican."* As we walked away I said to mother, I will have to get the DVD listed soon as it was near Christmas. I ended up selling it for over £35! I've still got my signed copy though, and I will never part with it!

Donations

When I first began selling I was often gifted items by family and friends to help me. You would be surprised how many people throw good quality items away. People often have a clear-out, so don't be shy to ask! When anyone is moving house is also a good time to see if you can 'help' them by taking items off their hands!

Storage

Yes, it's fine buying all this stock, but where are you going to store it all?!

If you don't have much storage space in your home or garage for stock, consider buying a shed for some extra storage space.

For information regarding storage units visit . . .

www.safestore.co.uk

www.ukstoragecompany.co.uk

Storage units are ideal if you have a constant flow of stock coming in and going out. However, if the stock is slow-selling, bear in mind that the cost of the storage unit could quickly cancel out any profit in the stock. Always keep your costs down to a minimum where possible. I would advise using all available free space in your home or garden shed before looking at storage units.

If you have the opportunity to buy stock that you know you will be able to sell on quickly ask a family member or friend if they have available space in a spare room or garage.

I have also managed to acquire stock cheaply from sellers who are clearing out a storage unit or garage etc. I once met a lovely couple selling a wholesale lot online. I was invited to visit their home and hand-pick the stock I wanted. He had purchased a huge wholesale lot and was hoping to sell off in smaller lots. We kept in touch and a few months later he text me and said he was selling the rest of the stock off as he needed his storage unit emptied that day. He offered me the whole lot for £300 and he would deliver to my house! The costs of storage units was eating into his profits, and he realised it was time to empty them. Another 'Del Boy' moment for me!

You can also bid on storage units. Visit the following websites for more information . . .

www.ibidonstorage.co.uk

www.titanstorage.co.uk

www.baggageauctions.co.uk/storageunitsuk

www.ukstoragecompany.co.uk/news/storageauctions

"A used . . . pink bathrobe
A rare . . . mint snowglobe
A Smurf . . . TV tray
***I bought on* eBay™**

. . .

Tell me why (I need another pet rock)
Tell me why (I got that Alf alarm clock)
Tell me why (I bid on Shatner's old toupee)
They had it on eBay™"

Lyrics from 'The eBay™ Song' by Weird Al Yankovic

10

Novelty Items to sell

I have given you practical advice regarding stock to sell on, however, you could also get creative and make novelty items for sale. By doing a simple search using the keyword 'novelty,' you will see a huge array of items for sale. I often look at these for inspiration! Some of the items are genius in my opinion.

Examples of novelty and creative items you could make and sell are . . .

Hand-made cards

Rude chocolate bar wrappers

Joke/ prank items

Survival kits

Craft embellishments

Wedding favours

Party bag fillers/ favours

Do some research and get inspired!

The Strangest Things Ever Sold on eBay™

You would be surprised how many strange items have sold on eBay™. The first item to ever be sold on eBay™ was a broken laser pointer. Pierre Omidyar (eBay™ founder) wrote the code for 'AuctionWeb,' and listed a broken laser pointer, selling it one week later to a laser pointer collector for $14.83.

Here are some more strange listings that have been listed on eBay™ . . .

A grilled cheese sandwich with the face of Virgin Mary

Believe it not this item sold for $28,000 in 2004. The grilled cheese sandwich was reported to have magical powers!

A ghost in a jar

A seller once listed a jar, which he believed contained a ghost. He claimed the ghost was terrorising it's owner. The description for the item stated that the seller *"would not be held responsible"* if the *"black thing"* escaped the jar, and that *"all sales are final."* The jar received numerous bids and finally sold for $55,000. Unfortunately for the seller, the winning bidder failed to make payment!

The meaning of life

In 2000 a seller from America claimed he had discovered the meaning of life. The final winning bid for 'the meaning of life' was, wait for it . . . . . . $3.26!

Britney Spears' Chewing Gum

A piece of chewing gum that Britney Spears had spat out at a concert in London during 2000 was retrieved by a lady at the show! She decided to list it on eBay™ and received an impressive $14,000.

A grandmother

'Annoying' but 'cuddly' grandmother for sale. You really couldn't make it up could you? This listing breached eBay™ regulations on human trafficking, so was taken down!

There are many more strange stories of historical eBay™ listings. A man once sold his entire life for $384,000 so he could start a new one! The winning bidder would be receiving the man's house, belongings, job and introduction to his friends.

An 18-year-old girl, from the UK, sold her virginity on eBay. She was trying to raise money to pay for her college fees. A kind businessman gave her the money she needed but did not take 'the service' she had offered!

An imaginary friend, a bag of air, unassembled snowman, and a human liver are amongst other strange listings that have been offered in the past.

"A daily routine built on good habits and disciplines separates the most successful among us from everyone else. The routine is exceptionally powerful."

Darren Hardy

11

A Daily Routine

This chapter is designed to give you an idea of an average day in the life of me, a full-time eBay™ seller.

Obviously the aim of being self-employed is to be able to enjoy the flexibility of running your own business around your lifestyle or circumstances. If you have children you will probably find running your business works best for you around nursery/ school hours, for example.

Structure your day to suit you. Some people like to make a to-do-list each day. You can then tick off each task as you go. Do whatever works best for you.

I share my daily routine with you to give you an example of how you can prioritise your business needs. The whole point of being self-employed is to help bring balance and harmony to your life. I worked in a Bingo Hall years ago which meant sometimes working up to 12 hours a day. I look back now at those times of my life when I didn't get to spend time with my family and friends and realise that I seemed to always be at work. My working hours affected my social life which meant I drifted apart from my friends. I did however meet my partner Gary while working at the bingo hall, so if I hadn't worked there we would never have met!

We all get a wake up time at some point in our lives, reminding us that life is too short! Why spend more time with people you work with when you could spend that time with people who matter to you? If you have the motivation to work for yourself, I say go for it! We all have hobbies or interests, so wouldn't it be great to make your hobby your job!?

When you are self-employed you have more flexibility to spend time with people you choose.

Here's an example of how I prioritise my day . . .

I normally start work at 8am by taking a cup of coffee to my office and switching on the PC.

Check my emails.

Log onto eBay™ and answer any queries.

Check the orders needing dispatching. I then pick the items that have sold. I have watched some people on youtube.com picking their orders and they have a habit of throwing the items in a plastic box. I can't see the sense of throwing items like this as you risk damaging them! I place each item on my packing table ready for packing.

Print the addresses using my thermal label printer and write on the back of the label the details of the item.

Take my labels to the packing table and match with items, then pack them ready to weigh them and print franking postage labels.

Once I have franked my items, I separate the franked mail into pouches supplied by royal mail. I will fit in my trip to post office or franked mailing box depending on my days plans. I always aim to post them by 4pm at the latest.

Coffee break! (many coffee breaks throughout day actually—that's the joy of making your own routine!)

Listing time. I try to list a few items each day if I can. After photographing my items to list I get started.

Depending on how enthusiastic I am for listing reflects how many items I get through! Some days I just cannot sit for hours listing so I go with the flow! I always set myself targets so as long as I meet my daily targets I choose what I do with the rest of the day!

If I am not in a listing mood I might decide to go shopping for stock. I like to visit markets and car boots so if there is one locally I will venture out! If I don't fancy going out I will spend an hour or so looking for stock online. Gumtree™ and eBay™ are my favourite sites to look for bargain job lots.

Sometimes I end up buying something for me or the house but as long as I get a bargain I'm happy!

The above is only an example, but the point is to show you how to prioritise. Notice my priority every day is answering customer queries and dispatching my orders. This is a must, every day. There are days when I don't feel like wrapping my parcels, but they have to be done. I owe my customers the quick dispatch I have promised them in my listing. Once I have finished my parcels for the day then I choose how I fill my day after that.

I believe if you want to run your own business you need to enjoy it. Then it really doesn't feel like work. That's how I feel the majority of the time. Trying to establish a routine for yourself helps maintain basic discipline to run your business successfully.

My business success depends on me. I am working to benefit myself and my partner, and obviously keep our cat Pixie in the life-style she has become accustomed to, expensive food, plenty of treats and a comfy bed!

People often say to me *"Don't you miss working with people?"*, *"Are you lonely working by yourself?"* Believe me, some of the characters I have worked with in the past is enough to put you off people for life! I love working by myself. I can now say I do not spend any time with someone I don't want to spend time with. How many people can say that?

"Please Mister Postman, look and see
(Oh yeah)
If there's a letter in your bag for me
. . . deliver the letter, the sooner the better."

Lyrics from 'Please Mister Postman' by The Carpenters

12

Postage options for business use

When I first began selling online I would take my parcels to be weighed at the post office. This meant long queues and often abuse from other people in the queue. So, I decided to register with Royal Mail's website and started buying stamp sheets online. This worked well for a while. However, I still had to queue at the post office to hand in my stamped parcels. The post office I regularly used was always busy. I knew the post lady quite well by now as I was there every day. Even though now I was dropping off the parcels, I still had to queue.

People assumed I would be there for ages getting my postage labels done for all these parcels. I often heard people complaining about me in the queue saying, *"we're going to be here ages, have you seen how many parcels she's got?"* Sometimes I just kept quiet and waited. My turn would come, and the post lady would smile at me and then walk over and open the hatch so I could hand in my bags. I would then turn and on my way out give the people in the queue a little smile as if to say, *"that didn't take too long did it?"* On some occasions while waiting in the queue a person standing behind me would look at my bags and then say, "*Would you mind if I went before you, I'm in a hurry and you're going to take ages.*" I would reply and say, "*That's funny I'm in a hurry too, the parcels are already stamped and just need to be handed over, so I think you will take longer than me.*" On one occasion an elderly gentlemen pushed in front of me and aggressively said *"I'm not waiting all day because of you and all them parcels.*" I politely told him I was only handing in my parcels, and I would not be needing any service at the counter while pushing myself back in front of him! It is really surprising how rude some people can be.

The bad experiences of queuing in a busy post office made me look at other options. I always made a note of how many parcels I posted daily. I could then estimate how many parcels I was posting annually. I then looked into different postage options for business users.

PPI (Printed Postage Impressions)

When your sales begin to increase and especially if you are selling online as your main income, you may need to look at how you can get cheaper postage. Once I decided I was unhappy going to the post office every day I found I could open a business account with Royal Mail and use a product called PPI.

Rather than going into all the details of how PPI works I advise you visit . . .

www.royalmail.com/business/services

Look at the products available and decide which one best suits your business needs. To avoid taking your PPI bags to the post office you will also need to arrange a daily collection.

Collection Service

I used PPI for a few years and also applied for a collection service. I was allocated a collection time when a postman would come to my premises and collect my parcels Monday to Friday. Prices change annually so it is best to look at their website for more details if you require a collection service. I paid for the collection service annually. However, I was getting cheaper postage using PPI than buying stamp sheets, and this made up for the cost of the collection service. I loved having the collection service it made my life so much easier.

I had 3 different people that made up my regular collection team and they were all lovely. I got to know them all really well. One of 'my' postmen was attacked by a dog during one of his rounds and was bitten so badly he had to have a skin graft and was off work sick for a while. During this time someone else took over his round so he never collected my parcels again. Over the years we moved house and I never thought I would see him again. Then one day the doorbell rang, and there he was with a parcel for me. We just looked at each other and hugged! I don't know what the neighbours must have thought! I told Gary of our encounter as soon as he came in from work just in case any of the neighbours had got the wrong idea! He just laughed when I told him.

For more information on the collection service visit . . . www.royalmail.com/business/parcels/collection

Franked Mail

After a few years of using the PPI service I was informed that I qualified for a franking machine. I looked into it and decided that even though you pay a monthly rental fee for a franking machine I would still be better off due to the amount of parcels I was sending annually. I now use a franking machine and the postage does work out much cheaper.

You cannot post franked mail in a normal post box unless it is inside a franked mail envelope. However, you can hand in your franked post at any post office or any franked mail post box. To find your local franking box visit . . . www.frankedmail.co.uk/post-box-location

For more information regarding applying for a franking machine I advise looking on www.royalmail.com/business/shipping and www.pitneybowes.co.uk

Courier Services

There are more postage options now than when I began in 2007. Here a few websites to look at for courier services . . .

www.myhermes.co.uk

www.parcel2go.com

www.parcelcompare.com

Tips To Remember

Use the most convenient postage method for you.

Look at different postage options. Would it be cheaper to use a courier service rather than sending through Royal Mail? Would a franking machine or PPI account save you money in the long run?

Always send high value items recorded delivery/ insured.

"Learn from the mistakes of others. You can't make them all yourself."

Usher

13

Scammers

I hear so many people say that they have tried selling online and gave up because they have been scammed in one way or another. It is very important therefore, to be aware of possible ways people can scam you online.

eBay™

There are many discussions between eBay™ sellers on the discussion board in the community section of the website. Take some time to read the problems some sellers are sharing on the discussion board and read the replies from other sellers offering help and advice on how to avoid being scammed.

This information will hopefully help you avoid being scammed in the way these people have. However, please don't let these scams put you off selling. I have been scammed in the past and it is not a nice feeling when it happens. However, I must stress that most buyers are honest. I have a saying that if someone scams me they will not get a second chance. The scammer immediately gets logged onto my blocked bidder list and are reported to eBay™.

I remember once posting an item out and I had a niggling feeling I should send it recorded delivery. I ignored my feeling and posted it out normal second class with no tracking. I always include my return address on the reverse of the parcel so if it was undelivered for any reason it would be returned to me. After a few days the buyer got in touch and insisted the item had not arrived and she wanted a refund. I asked her to confirm her address and I would look into this for her. After another couple of days, she contacted me again, *"Still not arrived, I want my money back!"* I was suspicious of this buyer from the start. I informed her that if the item had not been delivered it would be returned to me as I had included my return address. She replied, *"well perhaps your return address sticker fell off."*

How did she know my return address was a sticker, I could have written it on the parcel!? I immediately blocked her and reported her to eBay™. Always trust your instinct. If you have a feeling you need to send an item by recorded delivery . . . do it!

Scammers usually report their item missing really quickly and almost immediately demand a refund. If someone genuinely wants the item they purchased they will be willing to wait a few days for post and/ or give you the opportunity to send out another one.

There are many people who have been scammed online by sellers and there are many videos on YouTube™ regarding eBay™ scams and other online scams. Please take some time to view these.

Scam Emails

I receive a lot of emails apparently from PayPal™ and/or eBay™. Most of these are scam emails. Never respond to the email or click on any links. Never enter your log in details and passwords in response to the email. Log out of your email messages and log into your eBay™ or PayPal™ account. If the message is genuine there will be a message in your account for you to read.

What is a Phishing Scam?

Phishing usually happens via email but can also happen through text messages, social media and/or telephone calls. Cyber criminals use these methods to start communication with you with the sole intention to extort money or personal information from you. Replying to a phishing email may also enable the cybercriminal to download a virus which will infect your computer.

I cannot emphasise enough how important it is to take the time to educate yourself about possible scams. The more time you invest in researching how to avoid getting scammed on the internet, will pay off in the end!

"It takes a wise man to learn from his mistakes, but an even wiser man to learn from others."

Zen Proverb

14

Learn from other online sellers

You would be surprised how many online sellers have YouTube™ channels sharing their experiences. Some of these videos are very helpful and can provide some excellent knowledge that is passed onto you in a matter of minutes.

Learn from other sellers wherever you can. Their success stories can help you spot a bargain and their failures can make you aware of how to avoid making a loss in the future.

As I say, there are so many videos on YouTube™ with advice for online sellers. If you are serious about starting an online business please take the time to watch these videos and you will learn so much in such a short space of time. The advice available will help you avoid making some common mistakes, which will inevitably save you money. These videos will also give you a visual idea of how running an online business will be. If the sight of the stock and set up makes you anxious, then online selling is not for you! I often tell people my home is sometimes like a scene out of 'Only Fools and Horses' when Del Boy's living room is full of boxes!

When I was selling online as a hobby I remember going to meet one of Gary's friends who lived locally. Gary told me about his friend selling books online. I remember visiting his flat and being completely in awe at his set up. His flat looked like a secondhand bookstore with bookcases everywhere. He lived in a block of flats at the time. He was later evicted as his 'bookstore' was deemed a fire risk! But that's another story!

I knew instantly that I wanted to be an online seller full-time. Watching online sellers' videos will hopefully give you the same encouragement!

Type 'eBay' in the search box on YouTube™ and you will find hundreds of videos to watch. You might not find all videos helpful but it's worth going through them as you will definitely find some helpful tips.

I personally recommend Nic and Andrea Hill's YouTube™ channel. They have an eBay™ shop called 'The Hills are alive.' They have numerous videos uploaded. I recommend watching the following videos by Nic and Andrea . . .

'Car boot sale—bargain hunting'

'My day as a full time eBay reseller — Picking-packing-shipping'

'How to make an online store for your business'

Nic and Andrea upload regular videos on YouTube™ check out their channel for more informative videos. Of course, there are many more online sellers with YouTube™ channels worth seeking out. Spend a day browsing through YouTube™ gaining knowledge from other people's advice!

"Money is better than poverty, if only for financial reasons."

Woody Allen

15

Using Trade-In sites

If you would like to make some extra cash from your own items but don't have the time to sell them individually or have had no success in selling them you can always visit the following sites . . .

www.musicmagpie.com

www.decluttr.com

www.zapper.co.uk

www.webuybooks.co.uk

www.ziffit.com

www.cex.com

These are sites that buy second-hand items such as DVDs, CDs, books, games, and in some cases, electronics. Visit each site to see what type of items they are interested in buying. You will also need to read the terms and conditions before selling your items.

Most sites have an app you can download so you scan the barcode on your item for quickness. When you scan the barcode of your item a price will flash on screen that the site is willing to offer you. If you do not want to accept the price click on the remove option. Please note the sites above do not always accept all items you scan.

The site will have a minimum order for you to reach before you can commit to sell your items. Most sites have a free postage option. You may need to take your package to a collect+ store, or a local post office. In some cases, you can arrange the courier to collect the package from your house.

I have personally used all of the sites I have listed above. There may be other sites you can sell to, but I have only included the ones I have personal experience of. The sites above are very easy to use, and each have step-by-step guidance on completing your trade-in. They are also very good at completing fast payments straight into your bank account.

"Discard everything that does not spark joy."

Marie Kondo

16

Selling at a Car Boot Sale

This chapter aims to provide you with tips and advice on how to sell successfully at a car boot sale. You might find selling online is not for you, but you may still want to make some extra money from your unwanted items. You could also use a car boot sale to sell off some items that you were unable to sell online. Whatever your reason I am sure you will find the following advice helpful.

Find your local car boot sale using an online search. Always check if you need to book a space in advance. Most sales require you turn up on the day and pay for your pitch, however sometimes you can book in advance for a cheaper price. Check the weather forecast for the day you are planning to have a car boot sale.

Sort out good quality items first. Pitches on average currently cost approx. £10 per pitch for a car. You need to know you are going to recoup this cost. Use plastic boxes with lids if you can this will help protect your items if it rains. Fit as much in your car as you safely can. The more items you have the more chance of making some money. Don't forget a table. Pasting tables are a favourite to use as they fold away compactly

Take carrier bags and newspaper/ bubble wrap to wrap up fragile items.

Pack some old tablecloths and/ or waterproof groundsheet. Clear plastic is also ideal to cover your goods if the weather turns bad. Buyers will still be able to view your items for sale but the clear plastic sheet will protect your goods from rain.

Take a friend or family member with you. This makes the whole process easier for unloading your goods, displaying items quickly and dealing with customers. Try not to get engrossed in conversation with your helper though you need to be aware of customers. I have walked away from many stalls in the past because the stall holders have been too busy talking and not taking any notice of the buyers.

If you can, fill the car the night before the car boot sale. You will be required to be up bright and early, and this saves you some time. I would only advise filling the car the night before if you have the car parked in a garage or secure car space as you don't want to leave a car parked outside packed with loads of goodies for thieves to steal!

Take refreshments such as a flask of coffee/ tea and sandwiches etc. There are normally food vans at the car boot sales but taking your own refreshments will save you money.

Have a tub with a float. Give yourself a float of £10 at least in change such as £1 coins and 50p coins.

Set off bright and early and be prepared to wait in a queue at the car boot entrance as during the summer months car boot sales are very busy. You will be allocated your pitch by staff on site.

When setting up your stall don't be pressured by other sellers. Some sellers will leave their cars and not unload straight away as they want to see what other people have for sale. The general public are not allowed in until an allocated time so when you are setting up the only potential buyers are car boot sellers. If you are offered a price by another seller but you feel you want more just say no. If they really want the item they will pay the price you want or come back later to see if you are willing to haggle then.

Lay your goods out neatly. I don't know why some sellers can't be bothered to empty carrier bags and display their goods properly. When selling books, DVDs and CDs store them in plastic boxes with their spines visible to the buyers. Most buyers will scan over the stall quickly and a tidy stall will attract more attention. If you are selling clothes, try to display them on a clothes rail. Check how your stall looks to passers-by. If it looks too cluttered, tidy it up. If you have an unusual item place it in a position where it stands out.

Be friendly. Smile at passers-by and try to engage them in conversation. Compliment a potential buyer on their clothing or hairstyle. Your friendliness and charm could pay-off by drawing in the passer-by to look at your goods.

Price your goods, but also be prepared to haggle. Some people don't like to ask how much something is because if it is higher than they want to pay they feel uncomfortable. Make special offers if you can. For example, a sign saying 50p each or 3 for £1, draws the buyers attention to look at more items. Don't be too greedy at a car boot sale, people come looking for a bargain. If you are hung up on what you paid for the item brand new doesn't mean it's worth what you want for it. It's only worth what someone is willing to pay. As the time goes on and buyers are decreasing, offer more special deals. If you are having a clear out and really don't want to take anything home offer the whole lot at a bargain price. Buyers, who are online sellers, can sometimes grab a bargain towards the end of the sale.

If you still have items to take home and don't want to have another car boot sale why not advertise the lot on a site such as Gumtree™, giving someone else the chance to try their luck at another boot sale!?

"You can run a business any way you like, but you'll run it better if you build it around your strengths."

Duncan Bannatyne

17

Advice for business sellers

Once you have established yourself online and built up your feedback from selling your own belongings, you may now decide to make it a full-time business.

You will need to . . .

Change your seller account from a personal account to a business account.

Choose which type of shop you want to open if applicable. eBay™ have three types of online shops available: Basic, Featured or Anchor. Select the 'Help and Contact' page on ebay.com and type in the search box 'shop fees.' This will display a selection of search results. Select the 'opening an eBay shop' option to view subscription prices and listing fees. I would advise when starting out, to begin with a basic shop with the view to progress to a featured/ or anchor shop.

You may also want to change your eBay™ ID to another name which reflects the kind of shop you are going to open. For example, if you are going to sell mainly vinyl records and CDs, you may want to put something in your name that shows you sell this type of item.

Change your PayPal ™Account to a Business Account if applicable. Most sellers on eBay™ use the managed payments option now, however other sites may still use

PayPal™. If your business is going to be online and selling at markets/ events etc., you may want to apply for a PayPal ™card reader which means you can accept card payments.

Decide which postage method works out the cheapest for you. Check the products available for business sellers on the Royal Mail website and also investigate franking machines.

Start building up a listing of suppliers and contacts for stock, and packaging supplies. Regular research is advised to add to your list of suppliers.

Register on www.gov.uk as self-employed. Read the available information regarding Self-Assessment Tax return.

Learn basic book-keeping. Keep records of all income and expenses.

Think about marketing. Do you need a business card? Do you want to include leaflets/ flyers? Business cards are an ideal way to direct attention to your website/ online shop. Leaflet and flyers included with sold items are a good way to entice returning custom.

I can recommend the following websites for your marketing needs:

www.vistaprint.co.uk

www.moo.com

www.instantprint.co.uk

www.banana-print.co.uk

www.123print.co.uk

As your business grows you will find you may not always sell the same type of stock. Over the years I have added to my inventory depending on which suppliers I have found.

Remember building your business takes time and hard work. I have had a few requests from people over the years asking me to help them set up on eBay™, hence the reason for finally writing this book.

The funniest conversation I had with a friend (she will remain anonymous), went something like this . . .

FRIEND—Dawn Can you help me sell online; I want to do what you do?

ME—What do you mean? Do you want to pack your job in and work full time self-employed selling online?

FRIEND—Yes.

ME—Have you sold anything before on any online sales site?

FRIEND—I've sold a few things in the past.

ME—Selling Full-time is different to selling a few things over the years. You shouldn't pack your job in until you have built experience and know you can make the income you need. You also need to know if you are going to like it. Some people don't mind selling a few items online but it's a lot different to selling full-time.

FRIEND—I've had enough of my job and want to do what you do.

ME—I wouldn't advise packing in your job yet. Start selling online now and see how you like it over the next few months. If are making enough money to consider leaving your job then go for it! Once you leave your job you will need to register self-employed. If I can help you along the way just let me know.

FRIEND—Well that's why I need your help. I need you to tell me what to sell and where I can buy it.

ME—You need to do your own research and decide what you want to sell and then you need to find suppliers.

FRIEND—So can you do that for me?

ME—No, I'm a bit busy with my own business!

This conversation sums up some people's attitudes. You want to be self-employed and not have a job you hate. Great! The bad news is it isn't as easy as my friend would like it to be. She wanted me to give her a list of stock that would sell straight away and make her an income that could match her wage instantly. It isn't as easy as that. You will buy stock that sometimes won't sell but you will learn as you go. If you buy some stock that doesn't sell straight away try reducing the price or sell off as a job lot and try to claw your money back. Don't buy that stock again. I remember seeing an ex work-colleague while out shopping one day. He asked what I was doing now for work. I replied that I was an eBay™ seller full-time. He immediately said, *"Oh you can't make any money doing that, I've tried it."* I said it was going okay for me and I was happy. He looked at me like I was mad. He had tried selling mobile phone cases and accessories and found he couldn't compete with other sellers. If you are trying to sell stock such as mobile phone accessories make sure you can compete with the big businesses on eBay™ and other sites. If you can't compete you need to look for another line of stock where competition is not as intense.

The good news is that if you are reading this book you have already shown the initiative to take the first steps to sell online. The next step is up to you.

Whatever you choose to sell make sure you do your research. Build up your business at a steady pace that suits your needs and circumstances. I would also advise having a daily routine where possible. A routine can help you stay disciplined. Having a spare room as an office space is also recommended as you need to be able to switch off when you have finished 'work' for the day! Be prepared for long working days during the Christmas period as this is the time of year when there will be more demand for online shopping.

"You have to work on the business first before it works for you."

Idowu Koyenikan, 'Wealth for All: Living a Life of Success at the Edge of Your Ability'

You will constantly need to monitor the type of stock you are going to sell. You will sometimes need to sell off 'dead stock.' This is stock within your inventory that is no longer selling. Seasonal items such as Christmas items are an example of dead stock. Christmas is my busiest selling period however it is very important to be able to estimate how much you will need if purchasing an amount of seasonal stock from cash and carry outlets. Obviously if you have bought a job lot of seasonal items, as long as you make a profit on your total purchase you have not lost any money. The problem is sometimes storing the stock until, in this case, next Christmas.

I also recommend learning how to use the 'Time Away' option on eBay™ as you will need to use this whenever you are on holiday. You can also activate 'out of office' email replies using the 'Time Away' option. You may want to use this if you intend to only work certain days. Some people like weekends off. An 'out of office' email response indicates to buyers that you are not ignoring their message but are currently unavailable, and will respond when you return.

Another useful tool eBay™ have recently added is 'Markdown Manager' which gives you the opportunity to create discount voucher codes and sale events. I regularly have sale events and find these have been very beneficial to boosting sales.

I encourage you to continue reading eBay™ policies on a regular basis. Improvements are made to the site regularly and it continues to be one of the most easiest selling platforms to use.

Further Help available

I also offer a one-to-one tutorial programme and workshops. If you need further help in developing your business or advice on completing Self-Assessment Tax returns please contact me at materialworld123@yahoo.co.uk for more information.

I hope this book has inspired you to start your own online business . . . and always remember my favourite line from the Del Boy character in the TV show 'Only Fools and Horses':

"He Who Dares Wins"

18

Inspirational Quotes

Positive thinking is an important factor in life and business. If you allow negative thoughts to enter your mind, you will struggle to go for what you really want to achieve.

Here are a selection of some of my favourite quotes aimed to promote positive thinking . . .

***"I stand for freedom of expression, doing what you believe in, and going after your dreams."* —Madonna**

***"I've had a lot of worries in my life, most of which never happened."* —Mark Twain**

***"Being miserable is a habit; being happy is a habit, and the choice is yours."* —Tom Hopkins**

***"I may not have gone where I intended to go, but I think I have ended up where I needed to be."* —Douglas Adams**

***"The only place where your dream becomes impossible is in your own thinking."* —Robert H Schuller**

"Each morning when I open my eyes I say to myself: I, not events, have the power to make me happy or unhappy today. I can choose which it shall be. Yesterday is dead,

tomorrow hasn't arrived yet. I have just one day, today, and I'm going to be happy in it." —Groucho Marx

"The past has no power over the present moment."—Eckhart Tolle

"You'll never find a rainbow if you're looking down."—Charlie Chaplin

"Don't let someone who gave up on their dreams talk you out of yours."—Victor Hugo

"Don't be pushed around by the fears in your mind. Be led by the dreams in your heart."—Roy T. Bennet

"Faith is having a positive attitude about what you can do and not worrying at all about what you can't do."—Joyce Meyer

"Our greatest weakness lies in giving up. The most certain way to succeed is always to try just one more time."
—Thomas Edison

"The two most important days in your life are the day you are born, and the day you find out why."—Mark Twain

"There's no point in running away. Running away only wears out your shoes"—Del Boy

"Every problem is a gift—without problems we would not grow."
—Anthony Robbins

"There's no shortage of remarkable ideas, what's missing is the will to execute them." **—Seth Godin**

"Imagination is everything. It is the preview of life's coming attractions." **—Albert Einstein**

I hope the quotes above have made you think and hopefully inspired you.

Whether you are inspired to start your own business or change career, always remember to do what makes you happy. If you are working for an unappreciative boss or in a job that does not make your heart sing, always strive for more. This leads me to this classic quote from John Lennon . . .

"When I was 5 years old, my mother always told me that happiness was the key to life. When I went to school, they asked me what I wanted to be when I grew up. I wrote down 'happy.' They told me I didn't understand the assignment, and I told them they didn't understand life."

"You are the only one who knows what to do with your business."

Alan Sugar

19

Selling Categories & Suppliers List

This is a comprehensive list of eBay™ categories currently available at the time of writing this book. This list is provided to give you an insight into the categories you may choose to list in. With emphasis on how important it is to stock items that are going to be successful lines for you, please take time to research these categories online.

Collectibles and Art

Dolls & Teddy Bears

Art & craft supplies

Antiques

Stamps

Entertainment Memorabilia

Collectibles

Sports Memorabilia, Fan shop & Sports Cards

Coins & Paper Money

Art

Pottery & Glass

Electronics

Cameras & Photo

Cell Phones, Smart Watches, & Accessories

Computers, Tablets, & Network Hardware

TV, Video & Home Audio Electronics

Video Games & Consoles

Sports, Hobbies and Leisure

Sporting Goods

Art & craft supplies

Musical Instruments

Home Garden

Household Appliances & Supplies

Garden & Patio

Furniture

Pet Supplies

DIY Tools & Workshop Equipment

Bathroom fixtures, Accessories & Supplies

Celebration & Occasion Supplies

Home Bedding

Baby Essentials

Motors

Vehicle Parts & Accessories

Cars, Motorcycles & Vehicles

Fashion

Women's Clothing

Women's Shoes

Women's Accessories

Women's Bags & Handbags

Men's Clothing

Men's Shoes

Men's Accessories

Kids' Clothes, Shoes & Accessories

Costume, Occasion & Specialized Clothing, Shoes & Accessories

Jewellery & Watches

Business, Office & Industrial Supplies

CNC, Metalworking & Manufacturing

Office Equipment & Supplies

Healthcare, Lab & Dental

Material Handling

Building Materials & Supplies

Industrial Power Tools

Agriculture & Farming Equipment

Electrical Equipment & Supplies

Industrial Tools

Facility Maintenance & Safety

Industrial Hand Tools

Restaurant and Food Service

Test, Measurement and Inspection Equipment

Industrial Printing and Graphic Arts Equipment

Health and Beauty

Healthcare Products

Vitamins & Dietary Supplements

Medical & Mobility

Make-up Products

Hair Care & Styling Products

Shaving & Hair Removal Products & Equipment

Fragrances & Aftershaves

Facial Skin Care Products

Manicure & Pedicure Supplies

Oral & Dental Care Supplies

Bath & Body Products

Natural & Alternate Remedies

Media

DVDs, Films & TV

Music

Books, Comics & Magazines

As you can see you have a huge range of products you could sell. Decide which categories attract your interest and then source suppliers.

Suppliers

This is a list of online suppliers to help you source stock and packaging for your business needs. This is an example of some of the suppliers currently available.

Packaging

davpack.co.uk

globepackaging.co.uk

kitepackaging.co.uk

viking-direct.co.uk
pack-supplies.co.uk
packagingexpress.co.uk
lightningpackaging.co.uk
rajapack.co.uk

Stationery

stationerysupplies.co.uk
ryman.co.uk
staples.co.uk
wholesalestationers.co.uk
aosonline.co.uk
crosswear.co.uk
poundwholesale.co.uk

Wholesale suppliers / Online Cash and Carry

katiesstores.co.uk
wholesaledeals.co.uk
dhgate.com
clearance-king.co.uk
kdwholesale.co.uk
esources.co.uk
thewholesale.co.uk
andersonswholesale.co.uk
onlinecashandcarry.co.uk
budget-greetingcards.com
harrisonsdirect.co.uk
directdiscountclothing.co.uk

alanic.clothing.co.uk

alibaba.com

Obviously, there are hundreds of suppliers available. This is just a taster for you to see how ordering online and in bulk can help your business needs. Once you have decided in what stock you are going to specialise, you can then complete more research to establish suppliers.

"This time next year, we'll be millionaires."

Del Boy, Entrepreneur

Printed in Great Britain
by Amazon

79575559R00092